Shay logging locomotive
Douglas County Museum N967

Can't You Hear the Whistle Blowin'

LOGS, LIGNITE, AND LOCOMOTIVES

IN COOS COUNTY, OREGON

1850–1930

WILLIAM A. "BILL" LANSING

ISBN 978-1-7348046-3-8
Editor: Tom Hager
Design: Chris Michel

Cover Photograph:
The McDonald and Vaughn
Climax Locomotive No. 564
at Blue Ridge, 1914.
Coos County Historical
and Maritime Museum,
Jack Slattery Collection
992-8-0456

Special thanks goes to the
staff at the Coos Historical and
Maritime Museum in North
Bend, Oregon for the hours of
assistance in locating material.

Coos Historical and Maritime Museum 992-8-0705

TABLE OF CONTENTS

The Coos King steam donkey used by the McDonald and Vaughn Logging Company on Blue Ridge at the head of Daniels Creek in Coos County. Coos Historical and Maritime Museum Box H 37 989-P145

Prologue

My purpose in writing this book is to document this early period of Oregon history by outlining the construction, locations, and equipment used in developing the timber and coal resources in the Coos Bay area between 1850 and 1930, with an emphasis on the rail transportation that allowed their exploitation. When researching these topics, two important facts quickly became clear to me:

1. At the turn of the twentieth century, very few loggers or coal miners kept detailed records of their activities, their machinery, or their fellow workers. However, like most people, they enjoyed showing off their equipment to the camera. As a result, I spent a lot of time sorting through old photographs of steam locomotives and steam donkeys working in Coos County from 1870s to the 1920s.

2. Other books on the topic of short-line railroads are few and far between. Of those that attempted to illuminate the subject, I found, most fell prey to fact number one above.

I therefore freely admit and apologize for the fact that the chapters that follow contain far more photo documentation than they do narrative. I hope that despite this limitation, the book serves to illustrate and celebrate the early history of our region.

> Bill Lansing
> North Bend, Oregon
> January 2007

Libby Mine logging at Fish Trap Camp
Coos Art Museum

George Pike used oxen for skidding and horses to pull loaded carts down the level grade to a log dump on the Coquille River, circa 1902 Coos Historical and Maritime Museum Box 3 995-D115

Introduction

The westward migration along the Oregon Trail, starting in the 1840s, ended with most pioneers settling in the fertile valleys of the Columbia and Willamette Rivers and their tributaries. The pioneer population along the southern Oregon coast grew more slowly, and did not really get underway until the promise of gold brought prospectors to the area. The southern Oregon gold rush actually started in California with the discovery of gold at Sutter's mill in January 1848 before spilling over into the rivers of southern Oregon, where through the 1850s miners combed the hills searching for pockets of the yellow dust.

In 1850, a group of men calling themselves the Klamath Exploration Expedition left San Francisco to seek business opportunities and potential shipping and town sites along the southern Oregon coast. Following an unpleasant encounter with the Indians on the lower Rogue River, they sailed north and established a town at the mouth of the Umpqua River. It was called Umpqua City.

A year later, the small town of Port Orford was established, but not without incidences with the local Indian tribes. The white settlers persevered and the small town survived. In January 1852, a detachment of army recruits left San Francisco aboard the schooner *Captain Lincoln* bound for the military fort at Port Orford, but a winter storm blew them northward where their ship foundered on the north spit of Coos Bay. Rescue was delayed until the spring, but the returning soldiers spoke volumes about the area's potential, with the large and protected harbor they had "discovered."

About the time of the wreck of the *Captain Lincoln*, gold was discovered in the Upper Rogue River Valley and the town of Jacksonville was created. One year later, gold was discovered along the beaches at the mouth of the Coquille River in Coos County, signaling a possible gold bonanza upstream. Miners poured over the mountain

A mule team levels the railroad grade near Gardner, Oregon. Douglas County Historical Museum 13124

from Jacksonville and the coastal population exploded.

Oregon's Coast Range has always been an impediment to travel between the more densely populated central valley areas and coastal communities. In the early days, almost all transportation to and from the Oregon coast, both human and freight, was by ship. Struggling Oregon coastal communities were often tied more closely to San Francisco, four hundred miles to the south, than with inland Oregon towns eighty miles away.

As late as the turn of the twentieth century, access to Coos Bay was still difficult. Essentially there were three ways to get from Portland to Coos Bay. The preferred route was to take a schooner, usually the *Breakwater*, from Portland to Marshfield (which generally took two to three days, depending on tides and weather); the second alternative was travel by train from Portland to

The Coos Bay, Roseburg and Eastern Rail Road and Navigation Company's steamer Breakwater in Coos Bay. *The Breakwater* was the main transportation from Portland to Coos Bay before the arrival of the railroad in 1916. Coos Historical and Maritime Museum PC Box 4 000-14

the small town of Drain, Oregon, then by stagecoach from Drain to Scottsburg, where travelers could catch a boat to the mouth of the Umpqua River, then a stage along the beach highway—as long as the tide was out—and finally to walk a few miles across the north spit on the western side of Coos Bay for another boat ride across Coos Bay to town of Marshfield; and the third route was to travel the 200 miles from Portland to Roseburg on the Southern Pacific rail line, then take the stage from Roseburg to the Coquille River at Myrtle Point, then down the river to Coquille City where the passenger would catch a small boat and travel to the head of Beaver Slough where they would disembark and catch a wagon for the two-mile journey to the head of Isthmus Slough for yet another boat ride of some six to eight miles to the town of Marshfield. None of the routes were a pleasant experience—especially in the winter.

Supplies could also be carried across the Coast Range by mules. In the 1850s mule trains carried limited amounts of freight from Scottsburg, situated along the Umpqua River, to the southern Oregon mines. In 1869 another option became available when the Coos Bay Military Wagon Road was opened from Bay City, just south of Marshfield, to the inland Oregon town of Roseburg. Prior to the opening of the Wagon Road, pack trains would carry mail from the town of Roseburg traveling through the town of Myrtle Point and on to the Coos Bay area and its surrounding communities.

Despite the travel difficulties, the area's population continued to grow. In 1873, Coos Bay's Empire City was declared a US customs entry port in full anticipation of

the area becoming another San Francisco. Many investors wanted to be first on the scene.

Some settlers came with extensive financial backing, but few had knowledge enough to tackle the reality of capturing the abundance described by the early explorers. Familiar names in local history such as Henry Luse and Asa Simpson were successful pioneers in the lumber trade, while Patrick Flanagan struck it rich with coal.

As Coos Bay grew, the need for more efficient transportation became a necessity. But the steep hills and marshy valleys posed impediments to early entrepreneurs seeking to exploit the resources. Something else was needed: a way both to haul natural resources out of the rugged interior to shipping points miles away, and to haul employees, equipment, and supplies to work camps up into the mountains. What was needed were steam railroads.

The steam engine is generally considered one of the most important inventions of the Industrial Revolution. There is not one industry in today's world that does not in some way owe its success to the steam engine or its successors. The invention of steam as a power source was patented by James Watt in 1769 when he made improvements on a nearly century-old patent by Thomas Savery, who invented a way to use steam power to pump water out of a coal mine. In 1802, the first steam locomotive was built at Coalbrookdale, Shropshire, England, and the steam railroad was born. However, it would take another seventy years before the first steam locomotive reached Coos County, Oregon.

An interview of Mr. Ayre about his trip from Portland to Coos Bay in 1889 was reported by Thelma Lyons in the 1917 *Purple and Gold*—the Marshfield High School annual—entitled, "Coming to Coos Bay:"

Drain-Coos Bay stagecoach stopped at the wreck of the schooner *Novelty*. Coos Historical and Maritime Museum

"Could you tell me how to reach Coos Bay?" I asked of the hotel clerk in Portland. "Coos Bay!" he repeated as if he had never heard it before, "let's see, I guess you have to go to San Francisco first."

After several other inquiries, I was convinced that I should go to San Francisco. Of course I went by boat. It was just fourteen days from the time I boarded the ship in Portland until I stepped off on to the dock at San Francisco. But this was not the customary length of time, as we had smallpox on board and had to be quarantined. Besides, the sea had been extremely rough.

I soon found that Coos Bay was almost as unknown, tho' not quite as much in San Francisco as in Portland. All Coos Bay commerce, at this time was with San Francisco. Probably the best known fact concerning Coos Bay was that the miners at the Libby Coal Mine were on strike and therefore no boats were going to Coos Bay.

"Is there any other way I could possibly reach there?" I inquired.

"By taking the train to Roseburg you can get a stage to take you, if you strike it lucky," was the answer.

It didn't take long to reach Roseburg, and I immediately inquired about the stage. "Stage!" was the astonished reply, "No stage this time of year." I asked how the mail was taken in but was told that what mail there was taken by horseback.

I had practically decided to go by horse-back, when I happened to ask how my belongings would be sent.

"It would be impossible to take them in before June."

I was calmly informed. I determined to go some other way.

"Then you better go to Drain as there's a stage by which I could get to Coos Bay." I went to Drain. Before long I heard of a stage by which I could get to Coos Bay.

With two other men, I started on the stage. We hadn't gone many miles before the driver politely asked us to walk up the hill. So we walked up the hill and on and on. For the stage was never seen by us again.

We reached a sort of camp and stayed overnight. The meals were excellent. At this place we were very plainly advised to walk to Scottsburg if we wished to reach Coos Bay. We all agreed to walk the sixteen miles to Scottsburg. After partaking of another excellent meal we discovered an organ in a lovely warm room. I began to play and within fifteen minutes every man, woman and child of the camp was in the room.

At ten o'clock we were advised to "oil in" as we would leave at midnight. Accordingly, we were awakened at a quarter to twelve and left for Gardiner, traveling down the Umpqua. When we reached Gardiner, we were transferred on another

Early Coos County log train, circa 1900.
University of Oregon Special Collections PH10 23-ST25

boat to the ocean beach where we took the stage. After fording the river at Ten Mile Creek we reached a point on a spit of land opposite Empire City. Then having walked to Jarvis landing (across the spit) we crossed to Empire, by boat, at this time the county seat.

Most of the night, we spend sitting around a huge fire-place listening to bear stories.

Very early the following morning, we took a boat for Marshfield. This proved another tedious trip, but finally we were told we had reached Marshfield.

Thinking it over later, I found it had taken me just twenty-eight days to reach Coos Bay from Portland, but it was a trip I shall never forget.

Falling a big Douglas-fir tree in Coos County.
Note the length of the falling saw, commonly
known as a "misery whip" circa 1880.
Coos Historical and Maritim e Museum 974-68.11

chapter one

THE RICHES OF COOS BAY

Between 1870 and 1894, sixteen different companies
were organized in Coos and Douglas Counties for the
purpose of creating rail lines connecting Coos Bay with
the Willamette Valley. The chapters that follow delve
into the challenges and opportunities these companies
faced, sketch the character of their work, and detail how
the railroads that penetrated the draws and crossed the
marshy valleys of Coos County played a key role in the
success of the region. But first, since the railroads were
built for a purpose—the extraction of timber and coal—it
is important to set the stage by taking a look at the early
history of each industry in the region.

TIMBER

Logging has always been a story about transportation,
danger, and ingenuity. Whether it was getting men and
equipment to and from the forest, dropping the huge trees
to the ground, moving the monstrous logs from where
they fell to the mill, or getting the lumber from the mill
to the market, some form of heavy transportation was
required. In the beginning, Coos Bay-area loggers used
what was available naturally—the rivers and sloughs in
the region—to float logs to the mills.

The early loggers that came to the Coos Bay region in
the 1850s and 1860s discovered trees bigger than anything
they had encountered in the Paul Bunyan country of
Minnesota and neighboring states, where many of the
early Coos Bay timber men got their start. Saws and
rigging had to be fabricated to cut through the girth of
these giant Douglas-fir trees, commonly fifteen to twenty-
five feet in circumference.

One of the unexpected conditions of the timber in Coos

Old growth Douglas-fir forests of the late 1800s.
Yale University, School of Forestry and
Environmental Science

Steam Donkey

Dan Hepburn's logging camp on the Coos River. A steam donkey can be seen just to the right of the left snag, circa 1907. Coos County Historical and Maritime Museum Box 37 993-50.1

County, and for that matter much of the Coast Range of Oregon, was the extent to which fires had ravaged the native forests. Take for instance the comments contained in an article in the August 1902 Columbia River and Oregon *Timberman*:

> *The loss of timber by fire in Coos County has been enormous. It would not probably be far amiss to state in a general way that as much valuable timber has been burned as there is standing today. The history of these big fires as related by A. H. Hinch, one of the oldest pioneers in Coos, was to the effect that these fires were started by the Indians simultaneously at different points along the coast from Tillamook to the California line, in the [1850s] in order to destroy the rank underbrush and disclose the game. It is reported that the fire was so intense that thousands of elk and deer ran into the waters of Coos Bay to escape the conflagration.*

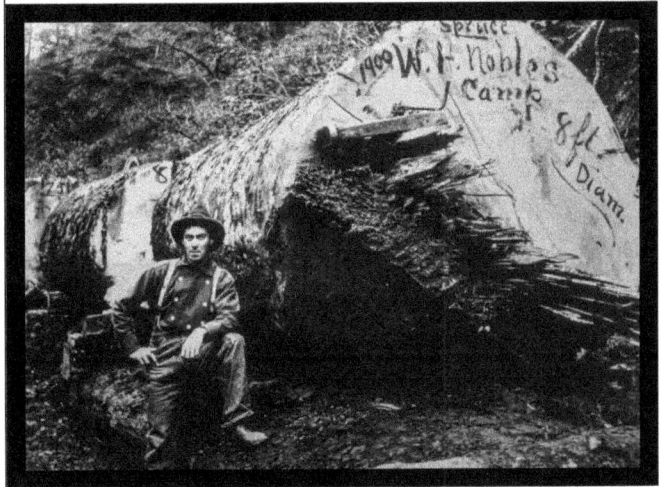

A log bucker shows off an 8-foot diameter Sitka spruce tree cut at W. F. Noble's Camp near Greenacres, Coos County, Oregon, in 1900. Coos Art Museum, Victor West Collection

A log bucker from the Noble Logging Company stands by a fallen Douglas fir tree on an operation near Isthmus Slough, Coos County, Oregon, circa 1900. Log buckers were paid around $3.00 per day in 1918. Coos Historical and Maritime Museum, Jack Slattery Collection 982-8-0404

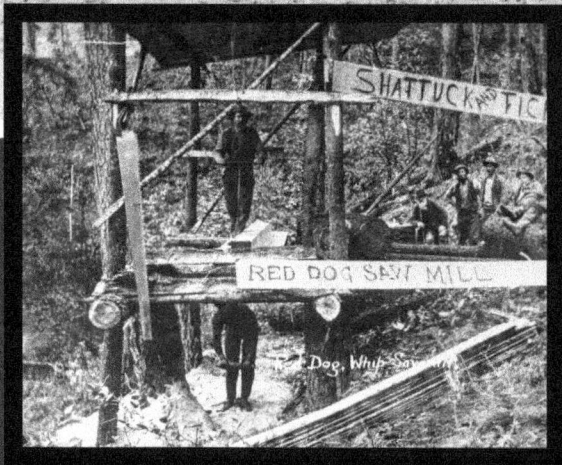

Whiskey Run gold dredge, circa 1910.
Coos Historical and Maritime Museum
Box 3 988-P14A

Pit saw at the Red Dog sawmill. Douglas
County Historical Museum

The lumber industry in Coos County began at the placer mining towns of Randolph and Whiskey Run near the mouth of the Coquille River. There the black-sand miners needed lumber for sluice boxes and were willing to pay almost any price to get it. That was back in 1853 when gold was discovered on the beach and miners were using animal hides or blankets to sluice it out.

A pit-saw mill was soon set up to manufacture the needed lumber. This was the first "sawmill" in Coos County—rudimentary but effective for small quantities.

Shortly thereafter, a group of three local miners by the name of Fundy, Stayson and Wasson bought a sash saw and put it to work on the Fahy property at Bullard's Beach, using water power from a local stream to run the saw. They were soon manufacturing lumber for homes and small schooners that hauled supplies to the miners working upstream on the Coquille River. Needless to say, the local pit-saw operators were soon out of a job.

As the area's population grew, sawmills were built by pioneers like J. Henry Schroeder, Edward Fahy, John Hamblack, Grube, Pohl, and Rink on the banks the Coquille River to meet the local demand for houses. The first "modern sawmill" on Coos Bay belonged to Henry Heaton Luse, who built a small mill on the flats in the area that would become Empire City. Luse first milled drift logs that were floating in the bay and its many sloughs. As sales increased, he was able to stabilize his business, increase mill production, and build a store and a wharf to export products. His initial cutting at the mill was about 10,000 board feet per day in a twelve hour shift.

In 1882, George Wasson had a crew of fourteen men logging near South Slough just down the bay a few miles from the Luse mill. He used a tramway (a "rail line" where the rails were small wooden poles held to the underlying logs by iron straps) about a mile in length to haul logs on a cart pulled by a mule. He could put about 12,000 board feet of logs into the water per day, for which Luse paid him $16 per thousand board feet delivered to his mill at Empire City. Luse also got logs from the Sumner, Oregon, area at the head of Catching Slough. These logs were floated down the slough to Coos Bay, where they were then towed to the mill by Luse's tugboat *Alpha*.

Bull team logging near Allegany, Oregon, circa 1900. Note the skid road that snakes back through the forest. Coos Historical and Maritime Museum, Jack Slattery Collection 992-8-0381

Spring boards were used on uneven ground so that timber fallers could work on a level plane. The "butts" of these large trees were significantly larger than the trunks a few feet above ground. Cutting them at ground level would make more work for the men. In addition, a log cut from the irregular tree base might hang up on obstacles as the logs were pulled from the forest during the ground skidding process, or create handling problems in the saw mill. Coos Historical and Maritime Museum H 15-967-126E

Even small teams of oxen could exhibit incredible strength. Note the beveled end of the log. Coos Historical and Maritime Museum 992-8-0389

Luse's chief competitor was Asa Meade Simpson, an entrepreneur from San Francisco. In 1856, Simpson established his sawmill at the edge of the water in "Old Town" at the north bend of Coos Bay.

His first efforts at cutting logs produced about 15,000 board feet per day. However, Captain Simpson was most notably known as a superb builder of ocean-going wooden ships.

While Luse sold his mill and land assets around Coos Bay to the Oregon Southern Improvement Company in 1883, Simpson stayed put and built quite a timber dynasty, passing it along to his son Louis J. Simpson. The first timber purchase made by Simpson in the area was at South Slough. It seems as though the younger Simpson was involved in just about every venture one could dream up during the time, but he never lost sight of his upbringing: timber.

By 1873, another sawmill competitor arrived in Coos Bay—the E. B. Dean Company. Dean rebuilt the Aaron Lobree sawmill on the east side of Isthmus Slough in the upper reaches of the bay, where he produced twice as much lumber as the Luse and Simpson mills combined. The demand for lumber was soaring in California markets as San Francisco continued to feed the construction needs of the gold fever boom-towns in the Sierra Nevada Mountains.

Coos Bay, with its vast timber resources and direct outlet to the ocean, was perfectly positioned to take advantage of the opportunity. Other operators soon arrived on the scene to test their skill at cutting lumber: Wilcox and Merchant,

Simpson's operation at Tar Heel Creek on Coos Bay, circa 1910. Douglas County Historical Museum 2470

J. F. Dunham, Pershberger, Cody, Moore and Porter, and a host of others.

Oregon loggers were an inventive, tough, hard-working bunch. The men who took trees down, the timber fallers, carried three main pieces of equipment in the early days: a falling saw, a double-bitted axe, and a spring board. On some trees with very irregular bases, obvious damage from earlier fires, or a tree with heavy taper to its trunk, fallers might cut the tree ten feet or more above the stump while standing precariously on their spring boards.

For the most part, oxen were incredibly gentle—given their immense strength—as seen here with the Hoffman brother's logging operation near Myrtle Point, circa 1910. As Nellie Hoffman Epperson Palmer recalls (currently 100 years old, shown at age five in this photo), the names of the bulls were Duke and Broad (up front), Buck and Ben (in middle) and Stub and Doc (in rear). The final animal was called Doc Number Two but is not hooked to the turn of logs. The bulls were fairly easy to train to pull as a team. Coos Historical and Maritime Museum, Jack Slattery Collection 992-8-0526

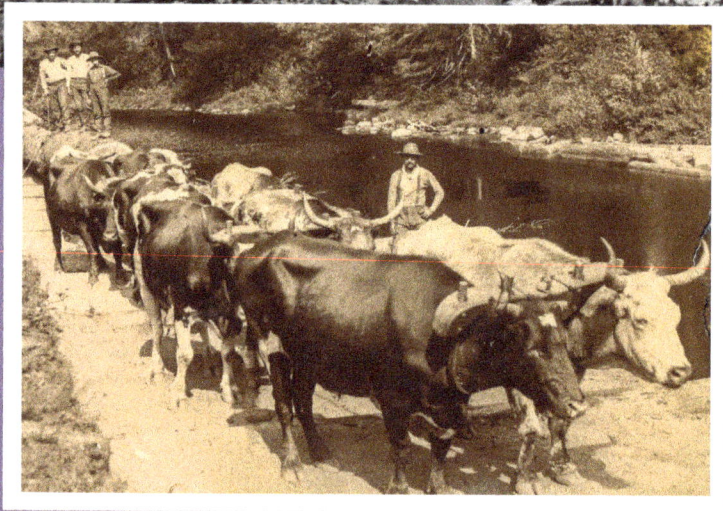

Bull team delivering logs alongside the South Fork Coos River, circa 1880, Coos Historical and Maritime Museum Box 42 987-P24

The combination of a bull team and a narrow gauge rail line made for excellent production when the timber was located some distance from a river or slough. Note the log carts behind the homemade locomotive, and how the logs are "sniped" or beveled on the end to prevent hang-ups when skidded by the bull team, circa 1895. Coos Historical and Maritime Museum, Jack Slattery Collection 992-8-0380

These boards, stuck into trees up to fifteen feet above the ground, were used to give the fallers a standing place well above the tree's often irregular or overly large base. The boards were four to five feet in length and about eight inches in width, tapering inward from an inch at the end to two inches where the faller stood. A metal flange with an angle spur was attached to the part inserted into the tree for added strength. The spur prevented the board from slipping out of the tree—most of the time! Maple and Douglas fir were the preferred species for the spring board. In 1918, a head timber faller's wage was around $3.00 per day.

Once these giants were on the ground, the task of bucking the tree into segments created a new set of challenges for the logger. The logs had to be cut into a size that could be moved to water for further transportation as well as handled by the steam-driven saws in the mills. Unless the logs were felled directly into water, moving them from the stump to the water's edge posed a major challenge for loggers. Oxen teams were the answer. The animals were brought to Coos Bay in the holds of ships or driven overland from Eugene or Roseburg. Their strength was incredible, and the sight of these teams in action was truly a sight to behold. The mechanism developed to connect the animals and the logs was quite ingenious. According to one observer:

A wooden yoke was placed across the necks of a pair of bulls standing side by side with a U-shaped piece

Two timber fallers in Coos County prepare to fall a large Sitka spruce. Note the height above the ground where the cut will be made. These fallers are at least ten feet above the ground and have used several spring boards to reach the desired height. Coos Art Museum, Victor West Collection

Bull team hauling a large Douglas-fir log on a homemade cart near Green Acres, Oregon, circa 1890. Coos Historical and Maritime Museum, Jack Slattery Collection 992-8-0405

Bull team/railroad logging Coos County, Oregon, circa 1890. Note the number of oxen in this team and the skid of logs behind them. The man behind the team is called the "bullwhacker" and the other men are greasing the skids to reduce friction. If a mill log became jammed against a skid, it was the job of the greaser to use a pry-bar to dislodge it. This team of oxen contained fourteen animals and could pull a tremendous amount of timber down grade. Coos Historical and Maritime Museum, Jack Slattery Collection 992-8-0396

The George Pike five-yoke bull team at Sevenmile Slough on the Coquille River in 1902. Coos Historical and Maritime Museum Box 37 989-P141

As long as wagons or carts were used and a fairly smooth grade made available, a team of horses could be used to transport loads of logs longer distances than the bull teams. Note the "reach" between the log bunks on the wagon. It employed the same basic principles as that used on the early logging railroad cars and much later on the diesel powered logging trucks. Coos Historical and Maritime Museum Box 33 989-P103.0

of wood called a "bow" placed under each bull's neck and fitted into two holes and held in place by a "yoke-key". A chain ran from a large ring in the center of the front yoke directly behind, then another chain to the yoke after that and so on until the last yoke was reached.

Each chain would be progressively larger as they went back. This assembly was fastened to the lead-log by a large hook called a "crotch-dog" driven into it. Where more than one log was pulled, they were hooked together using these same hooks and a short length of chain. This rigging was called a "coupling-dog".

Where bull teams were used to haul logs, corduroy skid ways or skid roads were built. Small timbers, eight to twelve inches in diameter and about eight to ten feet long made the best roads. They were placed just far enough apart so the oxen could get good footing and the mill logs being skidded slid from one to the next would not become stuck. These skids were buried cross-wise in the road such that the top side of each skid was a few inches above the dirt. All logs were barked so that the mill logs would "skid" across them more easily.

The normal yoke of oxen for logging consisted of five pairs for a total of ten animals. The size of the team depended upon the size of logs and the gradient of the skid road. If the road gradient was downhill, the team of oxen could haul six to eight thousand board feet per pull. This is equivalent to about two log truck loads today! If the gradient was flat, the team was limited to about five to six thousand board feet—still very impressive. Logs were

attached in single file, small end forward (if possible). All logs were "sniped" (tapered with an axe) on the end which helped keep them from sticking against the skids or becoming buried in the dirt.

The grease used for easing the friction between the mill logs and the skids was usually imported in barrels. Local bull team loggers however would use just about anything they had handy to ease the way, including rancid butter, bear grease, or tallow. The skid greasers (usually an entry level position in the logging company or the bull team owner's boys) often were required to sleep "outside" at the logging camps, during dry weather due to their "aroma."

While one might assume that the horse played as important a role out west with the loggers as it did with the cattle drives and the cowboys, it did not. The horse proved too temperamental for use in logging the steep canyons of Coos County. If a log got jammed sideways in a skid, the horse might rare up in an effort to continue pulling with all their might. This habit might hurt the animal, the handler, or other horses in the team. Bulls would stop cold in their tracks if the log hung up, awaiting a "switch" from the bullwhacker as a signal to keep pulling.

R.E. Scranton logging operation on Isthmus Slough near Coos City, circa 1889.
Coos Historical and Maritime Museum, Jack Slattery Collection 992-8-0393

If it were possible to reconstruct the total harvest of timber from the forests of Coos County over the past century, the original estimate by S. B. Cathcart (see chart at right) would shrivel by comparison. For instance, the Weyerhaeuser Company in the 1970s was harvesting over 300 million board feet per year from their forests on Coos River alone, and the Bureau of Land Management had an annual harvest of 250 million board feet per year during the same period. Other companies such as Georgia Pacific, Coos Head Timber Company, Moore Mill and Lumber Company, and Menasha Corporation certainly added significantly to the annual log production in the county. In other words, the timber harvest in Coos County in the 1970s was far more than the original estimate of 14 billion board feet by Cathcart a century earlier.

In the early days, logging camps were largely of the log-cabin variety or built from rough-sawn lumber cut at a local mill. The first units to be built were the cabins for the loggers; next came the cook house and finally the barns to house the oxen. Since the mills were all located on the rivers or next to the bay, and the oxen team loggers generally did not skid logs more that a mile from a stream, the early camps were usually built near water's edge—that is until the logging railroads came on the scene.

The problem with bull teams was that they were slow. Soon the demand for timber was outpacing the teams' ability to deliver.

The Emmett Pierce camp near Allegany, Oregon, circa 1900.
Coos Art Museum, Victor West Collection

In the August 1902 edition of the Columbia River and Oregon lumberman the following timber inventory in Coos County as reported by S. B. Cathcart is summarized:

LOCATION	TIMBER INVENTORY in million boardfeet
Saunders Lake -	
north to the Douglas County line	100
Millicoma River area	900
Lake Creek drainage north	
to the Douglas County line	100
South Fork Coos River basin	
west of Douglas County line	3,200
Davis Slough and Isthmus Slough area	200
North Fork Coquille River basin	2,500
Middle Fork Coquille River basin	1,500
South Fork Coquille River basin	2,500
South Slough area	2,000
Bear Creek, Lampa Creek and	
Fish Trap area	600
Seven Devils, Cape Arago,	
head of Kentuck Slough and other	
miscellaneous pockets	400

**Total estimated timber inventory
in Coos County 1902**   **14,000***

The percent of the different species in Coos County as reported in the 1902 report were:

SPECIES	PERCENTAGE
Spruce	5%
White Cedar	5
Hardwoods	3
Hemlock	5
White fir	5
Red fir	2
Yellow fir	75

* The author, Mr. Cathcart who was a timber cruiser at the time, indicates that if everything that would make a 2" x 4" x 8' board were cut, the forest would yield 18 to 20 billion board feet of timber.

The steam donkey loggers also utilized the rivers of Coos County to float their logs to the mills—that is as long as the timber grew close enough to the river. Here the Dan Hepburn operation along the Coos River pulls logs to water with a steam donkey, circa 1907. Coos Historical and Maritime Museum Box 34 993 -50 .5

Technology came to the rescue. In the 1882 a man by the name of John Dolbeer of Eureka, California, changed logging out west forever when he was issued a patent for developing the first spooling "steam donkey." Dolbeer's steam engine got its power from an upright wood-fired boiler attached to a single cylinder which drove a revolving horizontal shaft. The shaft was in turn connected to a turnbuckle or capstan, around which was wrapped a large cotton rope. The other end of the rope was attached to a log a few hundred feet away. As the spool began to spin, the rope tightened around the turnbuckle, thereby tightening the rope and skidding the log toward the machine.

The operation of the Dolbeer logging process required three men, one boy, and a horse—commonly white in color. One man, the "choker setter," would wrap the leading end of the manila rope around a log close to the skid road; a "donkey puncher," or engineer, (who might be required to actually assault the steam boiler with a wrench to get the system back in order) ran the mechanical side of the operation; a "spool tender" guided the manila rope around the spinning capstan with a stick—some tried to use their boot or hands only to end up with a serious injury; and a "whistle punk," usually a boy, communicated between the choker setter and the donkey puncher when it was time to begin to pull in on the rope. Once the log was pulled to an area next to the donkey the line was detached and hooked around a leather saddle "horn" on the shoulders of a horse that would obediently pull the manila rope back to the choker setter—and the process was repeated. The early steam donkeys provided no system to return the rigging

Tail block on high lead logging operation in Coos County, circa 1910. Douglas County Historical Museum N2669

Early steam donkey loggers—Fred Noah's logging operation near Allegany, Coos County—using a Dolbeer steam donkey, circa 1909. Note the lack of a haul back mechanism and the "fairlead" ahead of the spool. Left to right: George Noah, Fred Noah, Gus Wick, Charles Nelson with screw jack on shoulder, and unidentified man. Coos Historical and Maritime Museum, Jack Slattery Collection 992-8-0049

An unidentified logging operation at Fish Trap just west of Coquille, Oregon, circa 1890s. Coos Historical and Maritime Museum, Jack Slattery Collection 992-8-0444

back to the woods for the next log. The need to reach out further from the yarding machine and solve the haul back problem led to the development of the "improved" spool donkey about 1900 and the invention of "steel rope" or cable quickly found its place in the woods.

While the affectionate name of "donkey" was applied to these machines, donkeys were never part of the logging operation. In point of fact, the name donkey was coined by the local loggers in the region because Dolbeer's machine seemed too small to do the work required—much the way a team of burros would be incapable of pulling heavy freight wagons full of supplies over the hills. Time would certainly prove these old timers wrong. The initial Dolbeer Donkey and later modifications lasted more than a century and today remain a mainstay of the logging industry outwest, with diesel engines replacing the steam boilers and more sophisticated spools replacing the old capstans. These mechanical donkeys later became known as "yarders"— more accurately describing the process of yarding, or pulling, logs to a central location.

Coos County loggers quickly adapted to the new logging system and this new "contraption," combined with short-line railroads, put a rather quick end to logging with oxen.

A Coos County coal bed exposed at the surface can be seen here sloping from right to left. Coos Historical and Maritime Museum, Jack Slattery Collection 992-8-0724

The Bandon Block Coal Mine at Riverton, Oregon. Coos Historical and Maritime Museum Box H 33 S2-989-P102

COAL

Shortly after the discovery of gold on the beach at the mouth of the Coquille River in 1853, coal was found practically lying on the ground at several locations around Coos Bay and its tributaries, primarily along Isthmus Slough and the hills adjacent to the Coquille River near Bandon. The discovery of coal ignited great hopes for big profits supported by the industrial growth of San Francisco. Besides Coos Bay, the only other major source of domestic coal for the burgeoning hunger of the industries of California came from the Seattle region of Washington State. Coos County coal, it was thought, would have a competitive advantage being closer to the market—but, as it turned out, it did not.

As only time and tunneling would unveil, the Coos Bay Coal field had several elliptical seams that over eons had twisted, faulted, and dipped. The deep seams required tunneling, as the overburden of dirt and rock was (and still is) too great for any open pit extraction. Coal seams sometimes broke the surface of the ground, usually along hillsides, where locals would pick up chunks to burn. It was at these exposed locations that miners sank their first drifts.

Freeman Lockhart was one of the first to develop a coal mine on Coos Bay. In May 1854, he opened his mine and removed some thirty tons of coal. Perry Marple discovered another seam on his Donation Land Claim near Empire City and produced a full cargo of coal for shipment to San Francisco. Later a second cargo of coal was shipped from the nearby Boatman Donation Land Claim. Much of the Boatman coal was transported from the mine in wagons a mile and a half to Coalbank Slough and then transferred to scows for the trip to Empire City, where it was hand-shoveled into the holds of ocean-going schooners.

Boatman's first cargo was shipped on the *Chancey* and both vessel and cargo were lost on the Coos Bay bar—a common occurrence for those sailing vessels entering or leaving the bay. Early coal entrepreneurs not only had to face the dangers inherent in mining, but also the gales, tides, currents, and bars that threatened their shipping. From these intrepid beginnings, coal, Coos County and San Francisco would be linked for the next seventy-five years.

The geology of Coos Bay coal created major problems for miners, who sank deep shafts to follow the twisting seams. Mother Nature had a way of playing with the greed of these early local miners—many of whom had little or no experience with mining operations, but had substantial financial backing from investors in San Francisco. A typical operation might begin to dig into a hillside

The Newport Mine entrance. By the 1890s three portals were used to work the estimated six million tons of coal at the mine. The Newport Mine was renamed the Libby Mine after the post office was established. Coos Historical and Maritime Museum H 20-981-156

following a seam only to find after 1,000 feet of tunneling that the seam disappeared, moved up or down or sideways, depending up upon the earth's tectonics in the area. Available technology of the time did not permit the miners to do other than "guess" what direction to take. Many could only hope the vein of coal would be of sufficient width and length to make the expenses and dangers of extracting it worthwhile.

Not only were the coal seams of Coos County a bit fickle, but the mines also lay several miles from shipping points at Coos Bay or the mouth of the Coquille River at Bandon. In the beginning, there was no efficient way of getting the material to ships other than a long wagon trip like that described for the Boatman operation above.

Getting Coos county coal to any destination other than the local market was not an easy task. A few enterprising investors found success, but many others went broke. Two of the most productive coal mines in the county were the Newport (Libby) mine at the head of Coalbank Slough and the Beaver Hill mine at the head of Beaver Slough in the Coquille drainage.

Patrick Flanagan is a name connected with the development of the Newport Mine just south of Coos Bay. He came to Coos Bay in 1853 to hunt for gold, and managed to "strike at rich" on Flanagan Bar on Johnson Creek in southern Coos County, reportedly mining $20,000 worth gold—a sizable amount in the 1850s.

He used some of the money in 1855 to buy the "Newport" coal mine from Glen Aiken and his brothers, who had developed the operation to the point where they had shipped coal to San Francisco. Flanagan and Emerson Rogers purchased the mine, but Flanagan quickly bought out Rogers' interest and formed a new partnership with his brother, James Flanagan. As production grew, Flanagan needed help with the administration and logistics of operating the growing enterprise and brought in Samuel Stillman Mann from Fort Umpqua to handle the work. The Flanagan brothers gave Mann a third interest in the mine for his efforts. Together they worked it into one of the most successful coal mines in the area.

During the early years, all of the work in the mine was done by hand. The coal was shoveled into mine carts, pulled from the mine, dumped into a small bunker, then

Mule with cart excavating mining tunnel. Douglas County Historical Museum

into small rail carts that were pulled by a mule over wooden 4 x 4 tracks to the head of navigation on Coalbank Slough. Here the coal was loaded onto a "lighter" (small barge) which was floated down the Slough with the tide to a point near where Englewood now stands. There it finally made it into the sailing vessels that carried it to San Francisco.

As production increased at the Newport Mine, the tramway was extended further down Coalbank Slough by dumping mine waste between rows of pilings to make a solid ballast for the tracks (these form some of the dikes still seen in the area today). At the height of production one report indicated a labor pool at the mine totaling over seventy men. Soon a small town sprang up around the mine with a large store and houses built by the miners for their families.

An interesting point of history concerns the naming of that town: In the late 1850s and early 1850s, members of the local coastal Indian tribes were being forcibly removed to a reservation near Yachats, Oregon. As soldiers were scouring the area around Coos Bay, they came to the Newport mine looking for candidates to remove to the reservation. A well-liked Miluk Coos Indian woman known as "Libby," who worked in the Flanagan's home, begged Patrick Flanagan's wife Ellen Jane to hide her. Mrs. Flanagan concealed the woman in a covered flour barrel while soldiers searched the house. In 1890, when a post office was established and it came time for the small mining town at the head of Coalbank Slough to pick an official name, a decision was made to honor the Indian woman who had been so kind to early settlers: The

AREAL GEOLOGY
OF
COOS BAY COAL FIELDS, OREGON

BY J. S. DILLER, ARTHUR J. COLLIER AND JAMES STORRS

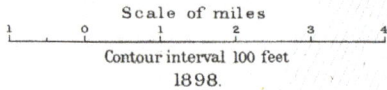

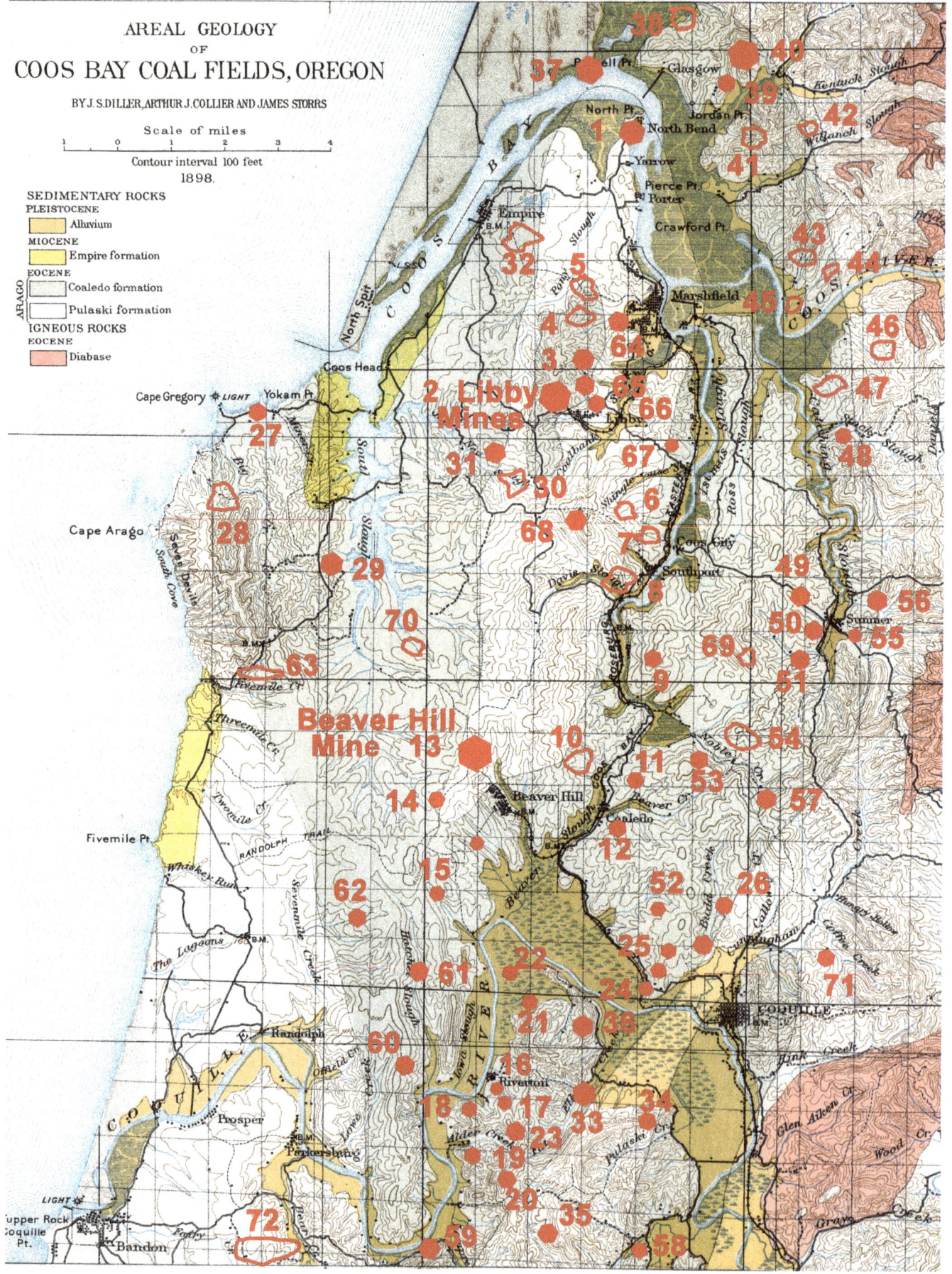

Scale of miles

1 0 1 2 3 4

Contour interval 100 feet

1898.

SEDIMENTARY ROCKS

PLEISTOCENE
Alluvium

MIOCENE
Empire formation

EOCENE
Coaledo formation
Pulaski formation

IGNEOUS ROCKS

EOCENE
Diabase

Libby Mines

Beaver Hill Mine

Cape Gregory — LIGHT — Yokam Pt.

Cape Arago

Fivemile Pt.

Coos Head

Empire

Marshfield

North Bend

Glasgow

Coquille

Bandon

Randolph

Prosper

Coaledo

Beaver Hill

Summer

Riverton

town was named Libby. Today, the community has been absorbed by the town of Coos Bay, but locals still refer to the area as Libby.

There would eventually be seventy-three coal mines officially registered in Coos County, and probably dozens of additional small, family-owned operations. For details, see the enclosed geologic map of the Coos Bay region (circa 1898) and the associated official mine registry reference. Readers interested in finding out even more about Coos County coal are directed to an outstanding treatise on the subject written in 1995 by Dow Beckham: *Stars in the Dark*.

But coal's story was just beginning when the Flanagans started their town. Almost forty years would pass between the time coal was first discovered near Coos Bay until the industry's full development in the 1890s. The long delay was due in great part to a lack of sufficient rail lines and locomotives for transporting the coal from the mines to the ships that would carry it to San Francisco. The same lack of rail lines hindered the timber and lumber industries. The Coos Bay area needed railroads to thrive. But they would be a long time in coming.

"Libby," a Miluk Coos Indian, seen on the porch of Mike Unilon's cabin. Coos Historical and Maritime Museum, Jack Slattery Collection 992-8-0665

The small town of Libby, Oregon, sprang up around the Newport Coal Mine, circa 1900. Note Newport Coal Mine Locomotive No. 2 pulling a load of coal cars destined for the bunkers at Marshfield. Coos Historical and Maritime Museum, Jack Slattery Collection 992-8-0675

REGISTERED COAL MINES COOS COUNTY, OREGON

1. Wilcox	25. McClain	50. West Prospect
2. Libby	26. Bituminous	51. Smith-Powers
3. Englewood	27. Yokam Point	52. Coaledo
4. Reservoir	28. Big Creek	53. Astandley
5. Flanagan	29. South Slough	54. Noble Creek
6. Southport	30. Oldlands	55. Newcastle
7. Thomas	31. Vey Prospect	56. Sumner Coals
8. Maxwell	32. Empire	57. Ferberish
9. Henryville	33. Masters Prospect	58. Hall Creek
10. Delmar	34. Lyons	59. Lampa
11. Overland	35. Albee	60. Donaldson
12. Martin	36. Hanson	61. Woomer Coal
13. Beaver Hill	37. Black Diamond	62. Sevenmile Creek
14. Klondike	38. Lone Rock	63. Seven Devils
15. Fahy-Muir	39. Glasgow	64. Archer Coals
16. Riverton	40. Gilbertson	65. Bunker Hill
17. Smith-Kay	41. Carlson	66. Belfast
18. Panter	42. Willanch	67. Caledonia
19. Lyons	43. Ward	68. Davis Slough
20. Sell Coal	44. Worth	69. 36-Coal
21. Eureka	45. Smith	70. Brown Slough
22. Scorby-McGinty	46. Lillian	71. Steinbeck Coal
23. Fat Elk	47. Gunnell	72. Bandon Coals
24. Cedar Point	48. Messerle	73. Lakeside Coals
	49. Huntly	

The first railroad built in Coos County ran from the head of Isthmus Slough to the head of Beaver Slough. The rail line was built by Gilbert Hall around 1871. The man in the dark suit is Gilbert Hall, the man with arms crossed is Mr. Lockhart, the other man is an Indian mule skinner. Coos County Historical and Maritime Museum, Jack Slattery Collection 992 -8-0185

Coos Bay, Roseburg and Eastern Rail Road and Navigation Company Locomotive No. 4 near McCormac log dump on Isthmus Slough. Coos County Historical and Maritime Museum 992 -8 -0285

chapter two

THE COMING OF THE RAILROADS

To help solve transportation problems that were hindering the development of timber and coal in Coos County, in the 1870s local entrepreneurs began to put serious effort into developing rail lines.

The first railroad in Coos County was the Isthmus Slough Transit Rail line, built by Gilbert Hall in 1871 initially to haul passengers and freight from the head of Beaver Slough over the low hill to the head of Isthmus Slough on Coos Bay. It followed the route of an old Indian trail, later used by early white pioneers living in the Coquille Valley. The Daughters of the American Revolution erected a plaque near the trail commemorating its existence. In 1876 operation of the rail line was taken over by the Coos Bay Union Coal and Navigation Company, spearheaded by William Utter, who extended it to the company's mine at Carbondale. The mine failed but the line was taken over by John Dunham who used it to haul logs to his small sawmill further down Isthmus Slough. By the late 1870s it had deteriorated to the point of being unsafe.

The early lines were as rough and ready as the men who made them. Many of the first steam engines used in the logging industry out west were homemade units. Since steel was difficult to obtain in the late nineteenth century in Coos Bay, several enterprising loggers built their own "rails" out of trees or lumber squared-up in a local mill. These were called trams or tramways. Wood was what they had, and wood was what they used. As noted in Chapter 1, the early logging camps were built near rivers or ponds out of logs or rough-sawn lumber, and the first railroads usually ended at the camps. Oxen teams were used to skid logs out of the woods to a central loading location where the logs were rolled onto specially designed

Early logging trains in Coos County were pretty rudimentary, circa Coos Historical and Maritime Museum H 18 S2-964-137G

Daughters of the American Revolution plaque commemorating the old Indian trail between Beaver Slough and Isthmus Slough. Author's photo, 2006

The "Transit Speeder" on the Isthmus Rail Road Line. It was assembled locally at Marshfield and was designed to run on wooden rails. It had a vertical boiler and was gear driven. Coos Historical and Maritime Museum, Jack Slattery Collection 992 -8 -0187

The Howell Camp of Sturtevant and Crane at Seven-Mile Creek in Coos County. This was one of the main logging operations for the Prosper Mill Company. Note the small steam locomotive and "trucks" used to haul the logs. Allen Leneve and Elmer McCue stand on the log at right, Harry Hunt stands by the engine, and Jess Nelson sits on the donkey's spool on the left. A bucking saw can be seen in the foreground along with blocks of wood that would be split for fueling the donkey and the locomotive, circa 1913. Coos Historical and Maritime Museum, Jack Slattery Collection 992 -8 -0436

A load of logs being transported to a mill in Coos County. Note the safety chains attached to each truck. Coos Historical and Maritime Museum, Jack Slattery Collection 992-8-0189

hauling carts, one log per cart, towed behind a small locomotive. The logs were generally held together, one to another, by chains, thereby forming a string of several cars heading down grade to the water dump. These logging engines were often "home-made" marvels, but they lacked much power to haul any heavy load uphill.

Even when the railroad loggers in Coos County first obtained the steel rails needed to modernize their short lines, the weight of steel forged into rails was much too light for heavy locomotives that would come later. Many of the first rail lines were the creation of the ingenuity of a logger of the time. The early logging railroads used "trucks" or railroad "dollies" to support each end of the log. This allowed the log to act as a center frame between the two units. This system enabled the trucks to handle even the largest of logs—sometimes up to 120 feet in length.

When the cars were returned to the logging site, each truck was connected to the next truck by a reach rod with a coupler. In the early days, these reaches were made of wood.

The Coos County loggers learned to increase production by combining the Dolbeer donkey yarder with the steam locomotive. Since the rail lines were built up the draws, the logs were yarded downhill. Techniques like this undoubtedly caused significant damage to the environment but there were no forest practices rules at

the time and few understood the need to protect the land for future timber production. Many saw the forests of southern Oregon as an endless sea of wood. Their goal was simple—get the logs out of the woods as quickly and as cheaply as possible.

Even as locomotives got bigger and the rails got heavier, loggers used the same technique of chaining the trucks together as they did on earlier lines. This technique allowed the logs to move around the curves without throwing the cars off the track. The same engineering is used by the modem log trucks, allowing them to traverse sharp turns on steep logging roads.

Counting the railroad that was built from Myrtle Point to Powers, there were at one time or another twenty-eight different railroad logging lines in Coos County. Many of the locomotives saw double duty, hauling both coal and logs on the same set of tracks, but under different ownership. Most of these rail lines were short, usually stretching no more than two to five miles.

By no means was building these logging railroads easy. Comparatively few of the operators used a steam shovel for excavating the initial grade. They were simply too expensive.

In 1918, a steam shovel was reportedly to have cost over $8,000 in Portland or Seattle—in today's dollars the equivalent of more than $580,000.

Typical incline with lowering/raising cable running over rolling pins in the center of the track. Photo taken near Rainier, Oregon, Coos Historical and Maritime Museum, Jack Slattery Collection 992-8-0316

A double-track incline of the Wisconsin Logging and Timber Company operation on the Columbia River. Oregon Historical Society Wisco 2551

The majority of the railroad loggers chose to use trestles not only to span draws and cross swamps, but also to get over uneven ground. The large trestles that were built to cross major canyons were truly engineering masterpieces of the sort that still survive time in the pages of old photographic libraries. But the true workhorse trestle in the west was the short trestle with piling (or bents) less than twenty- five feet in length and twelve to fifteen inches in diameter. Generally these were driven into the ground by steam-driven pile drivers as they built their footings across the landscape, two poles set vertically and the outside poles driven on an angle. These sets of four were placed about sixteen feet apart with timbers seventeen inches and up spreading between them. Cross ties were then attached and the steel rail spiked into place. Due to its rot-resistant characteristics, Port Orford cedar was the species of choice for the piling; when it was unavailable Douglas-fir trees were used.

Railroad logging spurs started at the mouth of a stream or canyon and progressed up the channel bottom keeping the grade as low as possible. Geared locomotives could haul the empty cars up an 8 percent adverse grade. But at some point the logger faced the daunting task of getting his railroad locomotive and logging men and equipment up to the ridge top where more timber was waiting to be cut.

Probably one of the most impressive yet notorious devices of the logging railroads was called an incline. As the rail lines reached back along the stream bottoms, they would inevitably be faced with a hillside obstacle that had to be crossed. There were two ways to do it: switchbacks, which took considerable time and expense to build, or inclines that were relatively quick to build and less costly—but far more dangerous.

Several different types of inclines Were employed to raise the empty cars and locomotives to the top of the hill and then to lower the fully-loaded log cars back down the track. The Coos King, for example, was a single-spool extra-large steam donkey equipped with massive brakes to slow the descending car load of logs—usually one at a time. This placed a heavy strain on the cable which on occasion separated and released the load down the incline, usually followed by a spectacular crash. Since these railroad log carts had no air brakes, workers would ride the load down

Early locomotive working on Hatchet Slough between Coquille and Bandon. Coos Historical and Maritime Museum H 16 S2 966-62G

the incline standing on the front and back trucks hoping beyond hope that the cable would not snap. Their job was to use a mechanical screw brake system to assist the lowering donkey by applying "brakes" to the wheels at the back and front of the load. Should the cable break, there was only one move available to the men—get off!

Another method of raising the empty rail cars and lowering the fully-loaded ones used a double-track system with a counterbalance—similar to an old fashioned elevator. As the loaded cars were slowly let down the incline by a donkey engine, another cable was attached to a weighted car coming up the hill. While this method was perhaps less dangerous, it required the construction of a double track, which increased the cost of the incline dramatically. This method was seldom used by Coos County loggers.

The other method of gaining elevation from the stream bottoms to the ridge tops was by using numerous switchbacks. This technique was expensive and much slower than the incline—but much safer for transporting the men, equipment, and logs from the camps to the rail lines at the bottom of the hill. Al Powers of the Smith-Powers Logging Company was probably the most inventive at using both the incline and the switchback methods while logging the massive stands of timber in southern Coos County. These will be discussed later in the book.

More details on each logging railroad operation in Coos County can be found in the pages that follow—some in much more detail than others. Research for this type of material is extremely difficult to assemble. The true knowledge of the ingenuity of these loggers rests with those who worked the steam donkeys and locomotives. Unfortunately very few of their stories have survived.

Sturtevant and Crane logging operation at Fish Trap west of Coquille, Oregon, circa 1890. Oregon History Society 5708

The Henryville Mine
on Isthmus Slough.
Coos Historical and
Maritime Museum
992-8-0677

The Coos Bay, Roseburg and Eastern Rail Road and Navigation Company Locomotive No. 4
delivering a load of coal to the bunker on Coos Bay, circa 1905. California Railroad Museum 15998

A "birds-eye" view of the town site of Marshfield with two coal bunkers visible alongside the ship channel, circa 1900. Coos Historical and Maritime Museum 985-28-27

COAL AND THE BAY

Logs were not the only product transported by rail. Coal, too, was important in the early development of Coos Bay railroads. Patrick Flanagan, who, as noted earlier, bought and developed the Newport Mine, was one of the early coal miners in the area who used steam. He eventually added a small locomotive to replace the mules that he had used originally to haul his coal from the mine to the shipping point. He capped the wooden rails with metal to gain better traction for the engine. While only capable of pulling four loaded coal cars to the bunker at Coos Bay, it was a significant improvement over animal power.

As mentioned earlier, the only real market of any size for Coos Bay coal was in San Francisco. A 1901 USGS report included the following:

> The coal shipped to California from the Newport mine is carried 4 miles, over a narrow-gauge railroad owned by the company, to tide-water bunkers, and thence by the company's steamers to San Francisco. The transportation rate is $2 per ton. Since the Coos Bay coal sells in the market for $1 less than the Washington coal, it will be seen that the former can maintain its place in the market only on a narrow margin of profit to the producer.

There are far more examples of failed mines in Coos County than successful ones, and the Henryville mine is a good illustration. As the story goes, a Dr. Henry had great plans to develop his 1,040 acres of cut-over timberland in the Isthmus Slough area. He raised an initial $200,000 in capital rather quickly from San Francisco investors in 1874 and began to lay out a town on the hillside above the Slough. Dr. Henry built a wharf with warehouses, a store, a boarding house, and a blacksmith shop, and built nearly one and a half miles of railroad track from the mine portal to his dock. He also built fourteen houses for the miners that worked in the mine. The town would become known as Henryville.

The coal outcrop at the Henryville mine was reportedly about seven feet thick but the coal seam had multiple layers of slate and clay. This was ignored by Dr. Henry and he continued to open the drift until he finally realized the coal was broken, impure, and essentially worthless. But investors continued to back his efforts and another shaft was dug some 400 feet down to reach lower coal seams. This also failed as they ran into bad air and the effort was abandoned. The shaft was allowed to fill with water. By May 1876, the site was abandoned. Several years later, another coal speculator tried his luck at the Henryville mine only to have a mine explosion dash his hopes and silence the mine forever.

The *Emma Utter* was a three-masted, 279.39-ton vessel built by the Hall Brothers shipyard for the Pacific Coast sailing fleet in 1875 in Port Ludlow, Washington. Her home port was in San Francisco, California. She carried the signal letters J. R. S. D. and her official number was 135205. A few of the known owners were; Pacific Coast sailing fleet, F. Gee, and E. B. Dean. The *Emma Utter* was abandoned at sea after striking a Grays Harbor sand bar on February 11, 1904.

Libby Coal Mine Locomotive No. 2, 1893. Coos Historical and Maritime Museum, Jack Slattery Collection 992-8-0668

Directly across the slough from Henryville on the west bank was Utter City—another coal prospect to go sour. Utter City once had a hotel (later moved to Empire City on scows; it became the Pioneer Hotel), stores (run by Henry Sengstaken), houses, and a post office. The town was formed in the mid-1870s by William Utter and his partner A. V. Ojeda. It sprang up at the edge of the slough with the idea that the coal extracted from the mine at Carbondale could be loaded aboard shallow-draft schooners from that location. A large sum of money was spent by the Coos Bay Union Coal Company at this mine, which was located four or five miles south of Utter City at a location that later became known as Coaledo.

On October 19, 1874, reporters from the Coos Bay News described a visit they made to the mine. One can determine from the enthusiasm of the news coverage that rumors about the opportunities for mining Coos Bay coal had run rampant:

By the time you get up to the Henryville mine, you find five strata lying on top of one another, making a total of 12 feet of coal in all. Here at the Utter mine, the tunnel is being run through a splendid vein 5 feet thick to tap another vein of 7 feet in thickness, the company of which indicates great hardness and density of coal. We have selected one specimen which shows fine grain in the lignite formation.

Further adding to the excitement at Utter City, two days later the same paper reported:

Utterville (Utter City) the terminus of the Isthmus Transit Railroad is now beginning to look like something. A spacious wharf and the boats land there each way. Five buildings have been erected there in the past fortnight and the air resounds with welcome din of the hammer and saw.

In 1874 Utter and Ojeda purchased the operation of the Isthmus Transit Rail Road for the purpose of transporting coal from their Carbondale mine. In order to do so, they rebuilt the rails and extend the railroad another three miles to reach the mine portal. The exuberant reporter of the Coos Bay Times noted:

It is just 5 miles from the mouth of the Utter and Ojeda tunnel to their proposed shipping point on Isthmus Slough opposite Henryville and to reach that

The *Breakwater* owned by the CBR&ERR&N is seen loading coal for fuel at a bunker in Coos Bay, circa 1900. Coos Historical and Maritime Museum H16-959-342E

point, these gentlemen are building a narrow gauge railroad and taking up the wooden rails of Judge Hall [The Isthmus Transit Railroad] tramway … The grade is quite heavy and in some places runs more than 100 feet to the mile. Where it crosses the divide between Isthmus Slough and Beaver Slough, it reaches a grade of 120 feet which is pretty big work for a ten ton engine … There are about 90 men at work. …

The highest bridge on the road is 41 feet from the bottom.

Herewith is yet another trivial, but interesting, sidebar to the time. Apparently Utter's partner Ojeda was a bit of an inventor as the following is reported in the Coos Bay Times on December 16, 1874 (in reference to extending the Isthmus Transit Rail line):

The use of hydraulic jacks in raising buildings and moving heavy machinery has been going on for some time, but A. V. Ojeda, of Utter City Commercial Company, has invented and is manufacturing a jack which works with whiskey instead of water and is claimed to be the most powerful of the two. These jacks are of two kinds—lifting and pulling. The latter have handles or ring bolts on them which can be adjusted to trees and stumps so as to pull them out by the roots. Most often the stumps on the line of the Isthmus Railroad were removed by these powerful little machines.

Locomotive No 4 of the CBR&ERR&N taking on a load of coal from the bunker at the Beaver Hill Mine, circa 1900.
Coos Historical and Maritime Museum photo 963-83D

The coal mining town of Riverton, Oregon, located on the south bank of the Coquille River. Note the railroad trestle accessing the coalbunker alongside the river. Coos Historical and Maritime Museum, Jack Slattery Collection 992 -8 -1942

The small towns of Utter City and Carbondale were built entirely on the premise that the coal mining operation would be profitable. Utter made plans to build an extensive railroad line all the way from his mine into Coos Bay and sent J. F. Dunham to San Francisco to obtain a locomotive—they called it the Isabella. Dunham shipped it to Coos Bay on the three-masted schooner *Emma Utter*. When the mine failed, Dunham purchased the Isabella and used it to haul logs along the same rail line.

By 1877, the Utter City-Carbondale enterprise was in deep trouble. Utter tried to recoup some of the railroad costs by hauling freight and passengers over the railroad. Ultimately this didn't work either. The mine was sold at sheriffs auction for $40,000 to a Colonel Fry of San Francisco, and William McCrindle bought the railroad; the railroad in turn was sold to the J. F. Dunham Logging Company.

Unfortunately both Henryville and Utter City became ghost towns when the ventures failed. The only evidence remaining of the Henryville operation are a few broken piling in Isthmus Slough where the wharf once stood.

The Flanagan coal operation at Libby also started using a rail line. Flanagan purchased a small locomotive for $4,000 in 1878 and built cars for hauling his coal to the bay. This was one of the earliest locomotives in the region. He extended the rail line farther down the grade and across the bottom at Libby, capping his wooden rails with steel to better support the weight of the locomotive as well as giving it better traction. The use of the train made their mining so efficient that they quickly extended the rail line all the way to the main channel on the bay.

The other successful coal operation in Coos County was the Beaver Hill Mine. Due to its proximity, the success of the mine was directly related to the construction of the Beaver Hill branch line of the Coos Bay, Roseburg and Eastern Rail Road and Navigation Company (which owned the mine). Owning a source of coal was a perfect fit for the railroad as the engine needed coal for fuel. This rail access connected with the main line railroad the company

built from Marshfield to Myrtle Point. Without such a connection, the mine would likely have failed. As the Beaver Hill mine developed, a thriving community sprung up near the portal, known simply as Beaver Hill, with houses built along six terraces above the railroad tracks. The community had a four-room schoolhouse with central heating and indoor plumbing, a store, a hotel, and many of the other amenities found in Marshfield. It even had a boxcar that was used as a make-shift jail, which undoubtedly housed many residents during the weekends.

Another section of the Coos County coal fields was centered around the town of Riverton on the south side of the Coquille River. This area was the southernmost extent of the coal field in the county. During the latter part of the nineteenth century several shipments of coal were hauled across the Coquille bar at Bandon destined for San Francisco.

Not only did San Francisco have an insatiable appetite for coal, it also had an abundance of capital looking for investments. Coos County coal miners shipped a significant amount of coal from their mines between 1860 and 1910. The last shipment of coal reported by the Coos Bay Port Authority crossed the bar in 1915. However a local market for Coos Bay coal continued to support small local operators for several decades.

Marshfield, Oregon, circa 1914, looking south over the town toward Coalbank Slough in Bunker Hill. Coos Historical and Maritime Museum 977-101.4

BEAVER HILL MINE

Beaver Hill miners, 1915. Paul Boyd center left.
Coos Historical and Maritime Museum, PC Box 1 973-62C

Beaver Hill townsite. The railway is the Beaver Hill branch of the Coos
Bay, Roseburg and Eastern Navigation Company Railroad, 1896. Coos
Historical and Maritime Museum, Beaver Hill Album

Beaver Hill School, 1896.
Coos Historical and Maritime Museum, Beaver Hill Album

Miners entering Beaver Hill Coal Mine, circa 1910. Note lunch pails.
Coos Historical and Maritime Museum, Box H1 981-244-15

Carts full of coal being pulled by horses headed for the Beaver Hill Bunker, 1896. Coos Historical and Maritime Museum, Beaver Hill Album

Miners coming out of the Beaver Hill Coal Mine, circa 1910. Coos Historical and Maritime Museum, Box H 981-244-21

One entrance to the Beaver Hill Mine. The man on the right is Oregon's Governor, William Paine Lord (1885-1899). Coos Historical and Maritime Museum, 992-8-0679

On August 12, 1893, the first train pulled into Myrtle Point and a grand celebration ensued. Passenger and freight service was now available for a fast trip on the twenty-three miles of track to Marshfield. Coos Historical and Maritime Museum, Jack Slattery Collection 992-8-0275

Coos Bay, Roseburg and Eastern Rail Road and Navigation Company Locomotive No. 1, manufactured in Cuyahoga, Ohio, in 1876. Coos Historical and Maritime Museum, Jack Slattery Collection 992-8-0283

As coal was being mined from the portals around Isthmus Slough, timber was being harvested from the hills surrounding Coos Bay and the Coquille River basin. Log rafts were built and floated to an ever-increasing number of mills dotting the shores of each locale.

Coal and timber gave Coos Bay its economic start in the 1850s and continued to dominate the region's economy for next 125 years. As both industries needed a similar overland transportation system to efficiently reach the deep-water channels at Marshfield and Bandon, the development of the short line railroads throughout the county would play an important role in further exploiting the resources. The locomotives used by each would change hands between the industries. But out of all these efforts and changes, one railroad company would assume special prominence in the region.

THE COOS BAY, ROSEBURG AND EASTERN RAIL ROAD AND NAVIGATION COMPANY

The CBR&ERR&N, incorporated on June 19, 1890, purchased the Isthmus Transit Line that ran between Isthmus Slough and Coaledo with the goal of building a railroad to connect Coos Bay with the Oregon and California Railroad line at Roseburg. The newly minted company's name was so long that local loggers joked that it took two boxcars just to carry the railroad's initials! The "Navigation" part of company's name came from the operation of a steamship line between Portland and Coos Bay that operated two steamers, the *Breakwater* and *Czarina*.

The concept of connecting Marshfield with Roseburg by rail was not new, but Robert A. Graham, the local manager of the CBR&ERR&N, had a different approach. He wanted citizens of each town along the proposed route to raise a portion of the funds needed for the construction. A few local pledges were obtained with the promise to make good on them once the rail line was well established and the properties along the route had increased in value. In preparation, Graham began acquiring property rights along the route in exchange for a "promise" to construct the connection between the two towns. No real money exchanged hands. Most of the contracts had a "give-back" provision should the company default on the actual construction.

The track, steam locomotives, cars, and other equipment required to build and operate the line were carried into Coos Bay by ship; construction of the first section from Marshfield to Isthmus Slough began in 1891. Progress was slow and money was tight. The third section of the line stopping at Myrtle Point was completed by the summer of 1893. The following, from the Orville Dodge history of Coos County (1898), describes the arrival of the first train into Myrtle Point:

> *The reunion of the Coos County Pioneer Association at Myrtle Point, Friday and Saturday the 15th and 16th will long be remembered by those fortunate enough to be present. The day dawned full of promise of good weather and when the last traces of morning mists had rolled away, the sun shone out with splendor that was indeed cheering. At about 10 a.m. the far-off whistle of a locomotive heralded the approach of the coming train with its precious load of human freight. The crowd in town quickly turned their steps towards the depot while many stopped on the bluff, others went down to the tracks to see, many for the first time, the cars coming into Myrtle Point. The train consisting of the engine and four cars was well loaded with people from Empire, Marshfield, Coquille City and other points [note: the track into North Bend would not be built for almost another twenty years]. The brass band came from Libby. The Myrtle Point band was on hand to welcome the crowd and conducted them to the public square. Here the procession was formed and headed by the two bands and marched out to Dixon's grove where the exercises of the day were held.*

It is little wonder that the citizens of Myrtle Point were in a celebratory mood. The CBR&ERR&N had just made the arduous trip to and from Coos Bay a fleeting memory. It also created a direct connection from Myrtle Point to Portland and San Francisco by linking the town by rail to Coos Bay, where passengers from Marshfield could board the *Breakwater* steamship for regular trips north and south. This was a major improvement over the first rail line built some twenty years earlier, which carried passengers only from Beaver Slough to Isthmus Slough following numerous connections with stage wagons and small skiffs.

The Beaver Hill branch line of the CBR&ERR&N was

CBR&ERR&N Locomotive No. 2 (manufactured at Cuyahoga Locomotive Works in Cuyahoga, Ohio, 1878) hauling logs at Davis Slough. Note the wide gauge of the rails, circa 1910. Coos Historical and Maritime Museum, Jack Slattery Collection 992-8-0282

CB&ERR&N Locomotive No. 2 crossing Davis Slough where it joins Isthmus Slough some six miles south of Coos Bay, circa 1893. Coos Historical and Maritime Museum, Jack Slattery Collection 992-8-0284

completed on August 22, 1894. Thousands of tons of coal were moved by the rail line from Beaver Hill to the bunkers on Coos Bay. When the demand for clear spruce lumber from the Allied command expanded in 1918, this branch of the local railroad would play an integral role in that effort (a section on the Spruce Production Division is located later in this book).

As the loggers moved farther and farther away from the timber stands surrounding Coos Bay and its estuaries and rivers, this rail line provided an efficient method for getting logs from the short-line sidings to the mills at Marshfield. It also hauled lumber from the saw mills in Coquille and Myrtle Point to the export docks on Coos Bay.

By 1894, however, it was also becoming clear that the dream of a connection between Roseburg and Coos Bay was not going to happen. The proposition to have the local citizenry help fund the project did not work, so along with a sizable amount of his own money Graham borrowed $500,000 from the Spreckles Company in San Francisco. He also continued to "spout the vision" of building the rail line all the way to Roseburg. As late as 1897 a message was still being reported by representatives of the CBR&ERR&N to the effect that the road would be completed to Roseburg. *The Myrtle Point Herald* quoted Graham on February 13, 1897, saying, "We expect to take up the work of the extension of the road to Roseburg in March and anticipate the line to be completed to that city in one year. We have all the necessary rail for the road on hand and plenty of funds to carry out the work." Investors relied on Graham's promise and, in the interim, relied on the connection to steamships departing Marshfield to earn the expected profits. But the project stalled at Myrtle Point for lack of funding. In 1898, the company along with its Beaver Hill Mine was in serious financial difficulty. Spreckles took over the operation, fired Graham, and brought in a mining engineer named W. S. Chandler. The planned link to Roseburg never occurred.

It is particularly interesting that the CBR&RR&N never did have a rail outlet to the rest of the country—that is, not until the Southern Pacific Company (or more precisely its subsidiary the Willamette Pacific Railroad Company)

The real pride and joy of the CBR&ERR&N Company was locomotive No. 4. Douglas County Historical Museum 9487

Four Hours Coos Bay to Roseburg

via two hours boat service, Coos Bay to Goodwill's, head of South Fork Coos River, from Goodwill's to Millwood, 20 miles via auto flange wheel car equipment over new steel track system. From Millwood to Roseburg, via auto rubber tire cars, over 20 miles present Douglas County roads, during the dry season, pending the completion of the steel track system through to Roseburg from Millwood.

COOS BAY AND WILLAMETTE TRACTION COMPANY.
G. F. Averill, President, Marshfield, Oregon.

Question? Are you the Marshfield businessmen and tax payers going to remain bottled up for another three years, rather than invest $100 each payable with a 12-months note, for the use of which you receive 8 per cent interest, payable semi-annually for three years, at which time this Company pays back in cash the par value of each preferred share with accrued interest to date, thereby insuring the success of the R. R. project that is absolutely feasible in attaining the results outlined herein?

Coos Bay and Willamette Traction Company
By G. F. Averil, President, MarshBeld, Oregon

As found on the back of the above post card with the statement to be in operation by July 14, 1911.
Coos Historical and Maritime Museum, Jack Slattery Collection 992-8-0274

Crossing the Bar at Coos Bay in the early 1900s
Coos Historical and Maritime Museum
PC Box 1-961-33.2

The bar at the mouth of the Coquille River was dangerous for sailing ships in the late 1800s and early 1900s. Here a Coast Guard lifeboat is being rowed through the surf while a narrow gauge locomotive builds the north jetty. Bandon Historical Society

connected the outside link from Marshfield to Eugene, Oregon, on July 24, 1916.

Until the Eugene line opened, overland access to and from Coos Bay remained difficult, leaving the Pacific Ocean the only route for moving products and people. Before 1916 the major cargo transported on the railroad remained coal (primarily from the Beaver Hill Mine) destined for the bunkers at Coos Bay, logs from the forests between Myrtle Point and Marshfield headed for the local mills, and general inbound freight brought in by ship. Of course, people could now make the twenty-six-mile trip between Myrtle Point and Coos Bay quickly, which was a major benefit of the line, even if not a particularly profitable undertaking.

Over time, the Coos Bay, Roseburg and Eastern Rail Road and Navigation Company expanded its fleet of locomotives. In 1906, the Southern Pacific Rail Road acquired the assets of the CBR&ERR&N for $339,555.22 in cash and assumed the bonded indebtedness of $625,000. With the purchase came the Beaver Hill Coal mine and rail spur to reach it. The SP finally built the long-promised connection to the Willamette Valley, but not through the Coquille River drainage. Instead, the company completed a line to Eugene via another route further to the north.

THE COOS BAY JETTY

Getting goods in and out of Coos Bay was a hazardous business in the early days. Ships and their crews had to get across the bar that separated the bay from the open ocean, a crossing that wrecked many a venture. The crossing was described by W. A. Goodyear in his 1877 treatise *Coal Mines of the West Coast*:

> *Every one of these river inlets (such as Coos Bay) has in front of it a bar of sand, upon which the water is not as deep as it is in the sloughs inside. These bars are ever shifting, and the deepest channels over them vary more or less in position as well as in depth with every heavy storm. The depth at low water on the bar in front of Coos Bay varies in different seasons from nine feet to thirteen or fourteen feet; and it is a most serious disadvantage to the Coos Bay coal mines that this depth is so small as not to permit the general use of vessels for transporting the coal which will carry more than three hundred to four hundred tons at a*

The two eleven-ton Baldwin locomotives used in the construction of the north spit jetty at the entrance of Coos Bay. The Yarrow is on the left, circa 1895. Coos Historical and Maritime Museum, Jack Slattery Collection 992-8-0731

Construction crane on the north jetty of Coos Bay. Coos Historical and Maritime Museum Box 23 965-135

A tug pushing rock barges for jetty construction on Coos Bay. Rock for the jetty came from local quarries on Coos River. Coos Historical and Maritime Museum Box B 996-42.5

A portion of the 3,600-foot tramway. This rail line approach was required to reach the beginning of the construction point of the south jetty protecting the entrance of Coos Bay. The barge slip on the inside of the north spit can be seen in the upper left. Congress authorized the north jetty repair at the same time the initial south jetty was being constructed. Coos Historical and Maritime Museum 992 -8-0743

Coquille River jetty construction.
Coos Historical and Maritime Museum 989 P233

The eleven-ton Baldwin locomotive hauling material for the construction of the north jetty atop the narrow gauge trestle. The centers of the trestle tracks were thirteen feet apart to accommodate two locomotives or one locomotive and the pile driver, circa 1895. Coos Historical and Maritime Museum, Jack Slattery Collection 992-8-0738

cargo. Moreover, in the winter the sea is frequently so rough that it is unsafe for vessels of any kind to attempt to cross the bar; and it has happened more than once that vessels laden with coal and lumber have been land locked in Coos Bay, and unable to get out over a month at a time.

In 1901, fortunately for the future development of Coos Bay, the US Congress approved a Corps of Engineers request to build two large jetties—a 9,500 foot structure on the north side of the entrance into Coos Bay, and a south jetty of 4,200 feet—and to maintain the channel depth at the bar of twenty feet during low tide. When completed, these projects greatly improved the ability of ships to call, but cost the government $2,466,000.

The initial work on the north jetty began in the winter of 1890 with the construction of the barge slip at the inside channel to receive the quarry stone. James Suydan Polhemus was the manager of the project for the Corps of Engineers. The Corps transported the needed stone via an elevated tramway or narrow gauge railroad atop pilings driven into the sand to form a trestle. By 1891, a short spur line was built crossing the north spit from the barge slip and the eleven-ton locomotive Yarrow had arrived by sailing ship, along with a large steam-driven pile driver. Polhemus constructed a double track rail line on the trestle with the tracks far enough apart to accommodate the two machines working in tandem. By August of that year, rock began arriving from a quarry on the North Fork of Coos

River. The north jetty was completed in 1901. It took eleven years from start to finish and used 637,000 tons of rock. In total, Polhemus's tramway reached a length of 10,368 feet from the barge slip.

Construction of the south jetty, which began the in the summer of 1923, immediately presented significant challenges to the Corps of Engineers. While the same design would be employed as used on the north jetty some twenty-five years earlier, a 3,600-pile tramway had to be constructed from the Charleston basin to the start of the jetty work.

Coos Bay was not the only local harbor to be improved. Coal seams were also being developed on the south side of the Coquille River near the small community of Riverton. In order for schooners to carry the coal to the San Francisco markets, they had to cross the treacherous bar at Bandon. There, the first effort at building a jetty on the Coquille River started in the early 1880s when a rock jetty was built for several hundred feet out into the Pacific.

Building the north jetty at Coos Bay, circa 1895. Coos Historical and Maritime Museum Box 23 965-135.F2

The Aasen Brothers logging operation at Rink Creek, Coos County, Oregon, 1906. Note the use of two spools—the mainline on the right and the haul back on the left. The horse is no longer needed to pull the line back out for the next turn of logs. Coos Historical and Maritime Museum, Jack Slattery Collection 992 -8 -0520

chapter three

THE COMPANIES

In the pages that follow I pay individual attention to many of the early logging companies that utilized railroads in Coos County. Within these entries, arranged in rough alphabetical order, readers will! see that some include more information than others. Research in this area is difficult for a number of reasons: Records are sketchy at best; and even more important, a true knowledge of the ingenuity of these loggers rests with the workers themselves, the men who worked the steam donkeys and locomotives. Unfortunately, few of their stories have survived. Still, by spending months picking through old files in historical societies, company offices, and government records, I found enough material to give at least a brief overview of many of the companies' activities. In addition, special attention is paid later in the book to two enterprises that, while not logging companies, had a great impact on companies working in the area: the Southern Pacific Railroad and the US Army's Spruce Production Division.

AASEN BROTHERS

The Aasen Brothers logged primarily in the Rink Creek drainage of Coos County between 1898 and 1920. They built a narrow gauge (thirty-six inches between the rails) railroad line that ran two miles up the draw. It connected to the Coos Bay, Roseburg and Eastern Rail Road and Navigation line at the eastern edge of the Coquille valley. The Aasen family homesteaded in Halls Creek area and the brothers built a rail line in that drainage for a distance of one mile. Later, John Aasen operated a logging railroad on Lewellen Creek near Norway, Oregon, in the 1920s. He also did some logging east of Reedsport, Oregon, about the same time, and had a logging operation on Middle Creek, where the company constructed a splash dam.

Aasen Brothers logging operation at Rink Creek, Coos County, Oregon, 1906, Coos Historical and Maritime Museum, Jack Slattery Collection 992-8-0515

Ed Aasen is wearing the white hat, 1906 . Coos Historical and Maritime Museum, Jack Slattery Collection 992 -8-0517

Aasen Brothers logging operation at Rink Creek, with company log train. Note the blocks of wood being split to fuel the boiler on the steam donkey and the locomotive. The skid road can be seen in the upper center of this 1906 photo. Coos Historical and Maritime Museum, Jack Slattery Collection 992-8-0521

Aasen Brothers logging train fully loaded at their Rink Creek operation in 1906. Note the fuel wood for the locomotive and the steam donkey along side the track. Coos Historical and Maritine Museum, Jack Slattery Collection 992-8-0521

AASEN BROTHERS

Aasen Brothers logging train at mouth of Rink Creek on the east side of the Coquille Valley, 1906. Henry Halberson is the locomotive engineer. Note the low trestle crossing the flats. Coos Historical and Maritime Museum, Jack Slattery Collection 992 -8 -0516

Aasen Brothers splash dam on Middle Creek, 1912. John Aasen is third from right; Ed Aasen is holding a peavey.
Coos Historical ad Maritine Museum, Jack Slattery Collection 992-8-0521

The *Martha Buehner*. Note the railroad trestle atop the north jetty as she comes across the bar at Coos Bay, circa 1918. Coos Historical and Maritime Museum PC 981-072

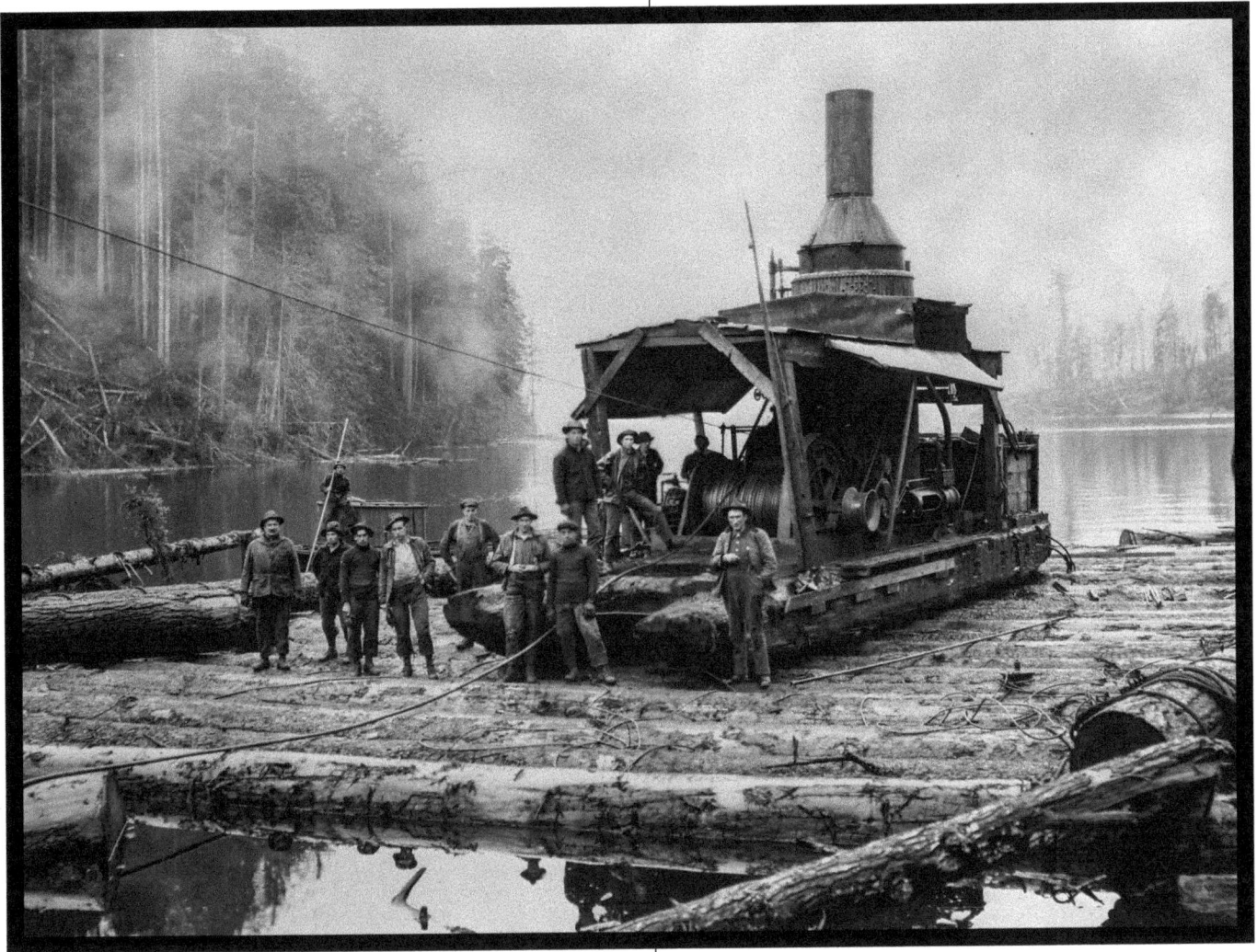

A Buehner Lumber Company steam donkey floating on a raft of logs on Eel Lake near Lakeside, Oregon, circa 1917. The mainline and haul back cables can be seen. University of Washington Special Collections, Clark Kinsey Collection 126

BUEHNER LUMBER COMPANY

In April 1916, Phillip Buehner of Portland, Oregon, purchased the Porter sawmill at North Bend—as well as the sash and door factory next door, some waterfront property, and 24,000 acres of timberland in Coos County—from the Simpson Lumber Company. Buehner also acquired the steam schooner *A. M. Simpson* and several lots in North Bend. In May 1916, the Buehner Lumber Company was incorporated and immediately began operations in Coos County. The company renamed the *A. M. Simpson* schooner the *Martha Buehner* and used it to carry their lumber between their mills in Coos Bay and San Francisco.

The company had several other tracts of timberland scattered throughout Coos County, giving them a total inventory in 1917 of more than 1.5 billion board feet. Without making any other purchases, they had enough timber to run their mill in North Bend for another twenty-five years. In the beginning, the Buehner Lumber Company

The Buehner Lumber Company logging camp at Eel Lake', circa 1917. The Eel Lake camp was well built, with three-room cabins for married employees. University of Washington Special Collections, Clark Kinsey Collection 127

operated two main logging camps: one on the Millicoma River near Allegany, Oregon, and the other at Eel Lake near the small town of Lakeside, Oregon. Both camps employed logging operations unique to each area. The Allegany operation combined a short line railroad with log rafting on the river, while the Eel Lake operation utilized a unique system of spar trees, cables, rafts, and locomotives to deliver logs to the mills at North Bend. Buehner also had a small logging camp in the Davis Slough area and later opened others on Black's Arm of Tenmile Lake and at South Slough.

For the Eel Lake operation, a logging railroad was built from the Southern Pacific line at Lakeside in a northwesterly direction around the hill to reach the logging camp at the southern shore of Eel Lake. This spur line allowed the company to bring logs from that camp directly to its mill at North Bend via the Southern Pacific line.

In 1917 work at Eel Lake was in a "hurry-up" mode as lumber was needed for by the Allied forces in Europe (see a section on the US Army's Spruce Production Division later in this book). There was a sizable quantity of high-quality Sitka Spruce growing on the hills surrounding the lake and the military needed all the spruce it could get for building fighter airplanes.

Buehner's logging system, designed to handle the timber growing on the hills surrounding the lake, was unusual. Eel Lake is a U-shaped body of water with timber on both arms, entirely surrounded by high hills. The system devised by Buehner delivered logs to the lake via a "tight-line/down-hill/gravity" technique. The operation included steam donkeys mounted on floats on the lake as well as others positioned on the tops of adjacent ridges.

Two spar trees were positioned up on the ridges—one close to the logging and another about a quarter-mile away at the very edge of the hill over looking the lake. Logs were yarded to the first spar tree by the usual high-lead/ground-skidding method which in itself had nothing to do with the gravity system. The logs were then "swung" to the spar pole at the hill's edge by another donkey in preparation for their ride to the lake. This was a rather simple mechanism as the logs traveled from one spar tree to the next along the same skid road. Once the log reached the second spar tree, the cable attached to the log (choker) was disconnected, the rigging pulled back to the first spar, and the process repeated again and again. Deep grooves were often the result of dragging these large logs along the same ridge path day after day.

The final step used by Buehner involved a third donkey floating on a raft near the lake shore. When a log was ready to be sent down from the second spar tree to the lake, the choker was reattached to a specially designed carriage (series of spools or pulleys) that rode on the mainline cable like a high-wire circus act riding a bicycle. When all was ready, the mainline was tightened and the log dipped over the edge of the hill, bumping down the slope. Then the mainline was brought up taut and the log cleared the ground. Now the carriage with its log in tow came careening down the hillside and the log struck the water at a high rate of speed. A special clasp automatically released upon impact and the log was contained in the boom. The

The Buehner Lumber Company logging operation on Eel Lake, circa 1917. Note the steam donkey on floats in the lake. The two work boats owned by the company can be seen to the left of the donkey. In this instance, the cable from the lower donkey is being used to move the logs into the lake. A box full of sand was sunk behind the yarder and used as a counterweight and anchor. University of Washington Special Collections, Clark Kinsey Collection 128

The Buehner Lumber Company locomotive at the South Slough operation, circa 1917. This locomotive became part of the transaction between Buehner and the Stout Lumber Company. Coos Art Museum, Jack Slattery Collection

carriage, pulled by the haul back cable, went back up the hill for another log.

This system permitted logs to be delivered every five minutes to the lake—if everything went well. When the logs were exceptionally long (120 or more feet in length) the choker was placed near the middle rather than around one end to prevent the long logs from dragging on the ground.

Frank Lyon, a native of Coos County and retired vice president and timber manager for the Menasha Corporation in North Bend, Oregon, remembered that when he was a youngster in the 1940s someone was taking "hemlock sinkers" out of Eel Lake. These logs would have been splashed into the lake by Buehner or Stout during the

early 1920s. Hemlock logs are notorious for not being able to float in rafts for an extended period of time—they sink! Since the cold water slows the decaying process, the logs at the bottom of the lake would have been pulled up twenty years later as sound as the day they were logged.

More than 350 million board feet of timber was harvested at Buehner's Eel Lake operation, according to one estimate. The company's logging manager, Mr. Sailor, said in 1918 that he was using twenty-seven miles of wire rope (cable of different diameters and tensile strengths) at the site—not counting the straw line—the flexible one-quarter-inch diameter cable pulled by men from the donkey to the pulley blocks near the back of the logging unit and returned to the yarder. The free end of the straw line would then be attached to the larger logging cables that would be pulled back into the harvest area for the heavy work.

Buehner also used a launch to transport men from the camp to the logging site at Eel Lake, and a larger boat to tow the log rafts to the landing dock at the south end, where the logs were lifted out of the water and loaded on rail cars. The larger boat also towed the steam donkeys riding on floats from spot to spot. This craft, the *Hercules No. 2,* fifty feet long, was hauled by rail car to the lake and swung from the car to the water. There Captain Wirth High, who claimed to be the admiral of the Eel Lake Fleet, took proud command!

Even today, some eighty years after this early logging operation stopped at Eel Lake, one can find the skeletal remains of piling poking out of the eastern arm of the lake where Buehner ran a log dump. All other evidence has been given back to nature as the lake is surrounded by a beautiful second-growth mature forest.

In March 1920 Buehner opened another logging camp on Black Creek at Tenmile Lake. A mile of track was built form the Southern Pacific line to move logs harvested beyond the head of Black's Arm to the main lake. Three logging operations delivered logs from the surrounding hills to the lake. The Black Creek camp employed seventy-five men and the Eel Lake camp employed 200 in 1920.

Buehner's third operation was located at the Gould Ranch at Allegany, Oregon. The ranch, purchased by the company for $7,000, was strategically located at the

The Buehner Lumber Company logging camp at Allegany, Oregon. Douglas County Historical and Maritime Museum 967

Buehner Logging Co. EEL Lake. Clark Kinsey Photo No 1

The steam donkey that was used on the ridge line above Eel Lake had to be moved off the log raft on the lake and pulled uphill under its own power—a very dangerous, but common practice. Once the yarder was in place and the spar poles rigged, Buehner's unique logging system would commence. University of Washington Special Collections, Clark Kinsey Collection 121

head of navigation on the Millicoma River. This became the company's base of operations for logging in the Marlow Creek watershed. Once the camp at Allegany was established, a logging railroad was built up Marlow Creek. From the rail line, logs were dumped into the Millicoma River at Allegany and rafted to Buehner's mill at North Bend. The Allegany camp had four miles of rail, two shay locomotives, and nine donkey engines.

Because the topography in the area is quite steep the company built two railroad inclines in the summer of 1921. One was 4,500 feet long with grades running 8-63 percent. The second incline was also 4,500 feet in length with grades of 20-55 percent. A Smith and Wasson lowering steam donkey was used on both inclines.

In September 1918 Buehner completed two and a half miles of railroad in the Davis Slough area. This line skirted the Boutin timber which had been purchased by the government for the war effort a year earlier. From this location Buehner could either transport the logs by rail to his mill or dump them into floating log rafts at Davis Slough or at Isthmus Slough for storage (later they would be towed to his mill at North Bend). The company

also owned a tract of timber it acquired from Simpson at the head of South Slough. The tract contained some exceptionally fine Port Orford Cedar, and Sitka Spruce that ran 8-10 feet in diameter. Buehner built a rail line into the property that traversed up Winchester Creek.

In 1922 the Eel Lake, Tenmile Lake, and Allegany camps were going full steam. At this time Buehner had 170 men working the woods and 210 working in the mills. The logging camps were producing 250 MBF per day.

In February 1923, the Stout Lumber Company purchased the interests of the Buehner Lumber Company. Local papers indicated that Stout would take over operations in March of that year. The Buehner mill (the old Simpson mill in North Bend) became known as Mill A. Stout also purchased the North Bend Mill and Lumber Company, which became known as Mill B.

The E. B. Dean Mill on the east side of Isthmus Slough, circa 1900.
Coos Historical and Maritime Museum H 18-961-139

Smith-Powers Logging Camp No. 2 at Eden Ridge, circa 1930. Coos Art Museum

C.A. SMITH LUMBER AND MANUFACTURING COMPANY, SMITH-POWERS LOGGING COMPANY, AND COOS BAY LUMBER COMPANY

No lumber baron had a greater impact on the timber industry in Coos County than Charles Axel Smith. This brief entry offers no more than a modest summary of Smith's operations; an entire book could be written on the workings of the interrelated companies he started in Oregon, California, and Minnesota.

Smith was born in the Province of Gatergoland, Sweden, on December 11, 1852. He came to the US with his parents, who settled in Minnesota in 1866. Later, while attending the University of Minnesota, he started working part time in a hardware store in Minneapolis for John S. Pillsbury. Smith dropped out of college to work for Pillsbury full time; in 1878 he opened a lumber yard in Herman, Minnesota, with Pillsbury as a full partner. Their business was known as C. A Smith and Company. As time went on the company expanded its operations to other towns in Minnesota.

The young businessman, on his way to what looked like great success, started a family. On February 14, 1878 at the age of 26, Smith married Johanna Anderson. They had five children (two boys and three girls). The boys went to private preparatory schools and graduated from Yale. Nann Smith, the oldest daughter, graduated from Smith College in Massachusetts; Adeline graduated from Ogontz School near Philadelphia; Myrtle, the youngest, graduated from Smith College as well.

In 1889 Smith bought out Pillsbury. He incorporated the C. A. Smith Lumber Company in 1893 in Minnesota, built the largest sawmill in Minneapolis at Camden Place, then started another company, the C. A. Smith Lumber and Manufacturing Company, to hold assets in addition to the mill. Smith became deeply involved in Republican politics and industry affairs in Minnesota. He served as a vice president of the National Lumber Manufacturers Association and a director of the Mississippi Valley Lumberman's Association.

In 1896, he carried a vote to the Electoral College for McKinley. Four years later he was a delegate at the convention that nominated McKinley and Roosevelt. He was also a regent for the University of Minnesota.

His sawmill ceased operation in 1912 as the white pine

Charles Axel Smith, 1909.
Coos Historical and Maritime Museum 990-34.

The Coos Bay Lumber Company Camp No. 2 at Doe Swamp near Eden Ridge, 1936, provided housing for 400 men. The houses were twelve feet by twenty-two feet, built on opposite sides of a common walkway. Each building had running water. The two camp dining rooms were thirty-two feet by sixty feet with eight-man tables. Each dining room was equipped with a full kitchen and bakery. Coos Historical and Maritime Museum, Jack Slattery Collection 992-8-0423

timber in the area became depleted. By then Smith was a wealthy man, owner of substantial timber holdings within the state, and well on his way to becoming one of the major lumber barons of the Pacific Northwest.

As the great forests of the Midwest shrank in order to satisfy the ever-increasing lumber demands of a growing nation, Smith, along with many other

The Smith-Powers Logging Company unloading a donkey from a raft at the head of South Slough at Camp No. 4. Coos Historical and Maritime Museum, Jack Slattery Collection 992-8-0463

Smith-Powers Logging Company log dump on the South Fork Coos River. Coos Historical and Maritime Museum, Jack Slattery Collection 992-8-0172

timbermen, headed West to stake out their claims to the vast forests in Oregon, northern California, and Washington.

The government was granting ownership to huge tracts of timberland for the express purpose of developing rail access to the region. Once the timber was cut, the lands were to be sold to settlers in small parcels. In 1900 Smith purchased 30,000 acres in northern Humboldt County, California, containing an estimated three billion board feet of redwood timber. In 1901, he began purchasing timberland in Coos County. In 1903 he bought 60,000 acres of sugar pine timberland in El Dorado County, California, with plans to build a railroad to the area from Sacramento.

The largest block of timberland owned by Smith covered parts of three counties near Coos Bay, where he accumulated a total of 180,000 acres containing an estimated timber inventory of eighteen billion board feet. In Linn County, Oregon, Smith owned an additional 45,000 acres containing an estimated four billion board feet. All the timber in Oregon was held by the C. A. Smith Timber Company, an Oregon corporation. The C. A. Smith Lumber and Manufacturing Company was also licensed to do business in the state of Oregon in 1907. The directors of the company were listed as C. A. Smith, Charles L. Trabert and Lyman E. Minor.

In February 1907 Smith purchased sixty acres of land at the mouth of Isthmus Slough from the Flanagan family of Marshfield. He next acquired the old Adam Lobree mill on the east side of the Slough, which was owned by the E. B. Dean Company (a partnership composed of E. B. Dean, David Wilcox and C. H. Merchant). There Smith cut the lumber he needed to construct one of the biggest sawmills in the Pacific Northwest, which he built on the newly acquired Flanagan parcel. The mill was a marvel of its day, equipped with electric lights, a sprinkler system, a three-story office building with a second-floor restaurant and third-floor apartments for the men, a billiard room, and a bowling alley in the basement. All the rooms were sided with the various woods of Coos County.

When Smith acquired the E. B. Dean Company mill, he also purchased Dean's extensive timber holdings and a railroad. The property—10,000 acres with an old-growth timber inventory of more than 250 MBF—was located on Cunningham Creek around the small community of Fairview. The purchase also included some 1,500 acres of coal land near the present site of Del Mar on the west side of Isthmus Slough. The Dean land, along with the large tracts of government land acquired around Eden Ridge, provided Smith a vast reservoir of large fine-grained timber. With all that land came the clear need for an extensive rail system.

As was a common practice at the time, Smith organized each of his business ventures into separate entities. In 1907, these included:

- Inter-Ocean Transportation Company

- The Marshfield Realty and Trading Company
- Smith-Powers Logging Company (C. A. Smith, Albert H. Powers and Charles L. Trabert subscribers—a Minnesota corporation in 1907).
- Pacific States Timber Investment Company
- Coos Bay Lumber Company (Rupert Irwin, Albert H. Powers, Vemon A. Smith subscribers formed in 1914)
- C. A. Smith Timber Company (Vemon Smith, David Nelson and Albert H. Powers subscribers—a Minnesota corporation in 1915)
- C. A. Smith Fir Company (C. A. Smith, Johanna Smith and John Lind subscribers—a Minnesota corporation in 1906)
- C. A. Smith Land Company

Later he also formed Western Lumber and Manufacturing with his son Carrol Smith. This company used Port Orford Cedar waste products from the big sawmill on Isthmus Slough. The "scrap" pieces of lumber went into window blinds, window sashes and washboard stock that were in high demand in the east.

In 1912, the Coos Bay Pulp and Paper Company was formed, with C. A. Smith president, Vemon Smith (his other son) vice president, Charles L. Trabert secretary, Hjalta Nerdrum treasurer, and Rolh Nerdrum superintendent. The pulp mill was built adjacent to the big sawmill on Isthmus Slough. Construction started in 1913. First, waste from the sawmill was ground and used to fill the lowlands. After that, the waste was used to fuel the boiler to create steam at the pulp mill. The pulp plant cost $500,000 to build with capacity of forty tons a day. Saltwater was pumped from the bay and ran through a filtering system with a capacity of four million gallons per day. The market for the pulp was Japan and China. But the operation never really made money. In May 1916 the operation was closed and the machinery sold to Crown Willamette Paper Company in Oregon City. The other major player in Smith's expanding empire was Albert Henry Powers. Bom in a log cabin in Ontario, Canada, on November 6, 1861 (both his parents were US citizens), Powers was sixteen years old when he went work in to a logging camp in Michigan. By the age of twenty-one he had started his own logging operation in Hibbing, Minnesota, where he built a growing business over the next twenty-four years. It was reported that at one time he owned more than 400 horses (used to skid the loaded sleds full of logs over the frozen forest roads to the mill). Powers also built a twenty-eight-mile-long railroad connecting his logging camp with the town of Hibbing. His camp grew into a small town in its own right and carried his name, but as with so many logging communities it drifted into history: Powers, Minnesota, no longer exists.

Carroll and Vemon Smith, sons of C. A. Smith.

While many of the logging railroads in the region were laid out by a woods boss, some companies used survey crews to establish the grade once the logging manager determined the destination. Frank Segur and George A. Dwyer, logging engineers for the Smith-Powers Logging Company, were graduates of the Great Northern engineering department. They were responsible for building the rail lines up Eden Ridge and Salmon Creek. Coos Historical and Maritime Museum H18-966-87D

Powers was also a joint owner of the Powers-Simpson Logging Company in Hibbing, which supplied logs to C. A. Smith's mill in Minneapolis. It was through that relationship that a business-friendship was born between these two men. Both Smith and Powers knew their future in timber did not lie in the diminishing forests of the Midwest. Smith had traveled extensively out West and realized that given the government's ridiculously cheap price for timberlands, investments in the area seemed like a sure thing (for a detailed treatise on the timber and railroad land practices of the day, readers are directed to Steven Douglas Puter's 1908 book Looters of the Public Domain).

Smith was a financier and mill operator, not a logger. So he talked an ambitious logger, Al Powers, into joining his Oregon ventures. In September 1907 Powers moved his large family (wife Johanna and six children) to Marshfield, Oregon, where he became vice president and general manager of the Smith-Powers Logging Company. It was reported that the trip West required two boxcars to transport Power's household goods and animals, which included a white Stanley Steamer car, a team of horses, a surrey with a fringe on top, and three English dogs. They left the transcontinental train in Portland and boarded the steamer *Breakwater* for the final leg of the journey to Coos Bay, where Powers built a home for his family on Hall Street in Marshfield (today it is a bed and breakfast facility). His oldest son, Fred, immediately joined his father in the logging camps. When the senior Powers left the company in the early 1920s, Fred became manager of the logging operation. Powers' younger son Albert, Jr. followed an interest in cattle ranching and was never connected with the Smith-Powers Logging Company business.

Together Smith and Powers built a timber dynasty in Coos County that would last for a decade—and would become one of the largest logging/railroad/sawmilling/pulp mill operations in the United States. Smith took charge of the milling, sales, and shipping, while Powers handled the logging, railroad, and rafting operations. A new company was incorporated in January 1907—The Smith-Powers Logging Company—with the sole purpose of logging the timber owned by the C. A. Smith Timber Company and supplying logs from those lands mill owned by the C. A. Smith Lumber and Manufacturing Company. From 1907 to 1911, it was reported by the American Lumberman that the company logged 425 million board feet of timber in 1911 with an average production of more than 1.3 MBF per day.

Much has been written about how Smith and Powers were ahead of their times in sawmill and logging technologies, but little has been said about Smith's pioneering interest in maintaining his timberlands after they were logged. In fact, Smith maintained a forestry department at his Coos Bay operation supervised by John Lafon, Jr. His companies' forestry activity included marking one seed tree per acre (usually a defective old growth Douglas fir), protecting it during the logging operation, and burning the logging debris in the spring or fall following, taking special care not to damage the seed tree. The result was reforestation—even if it was "hit or miss." In addition, Lafon maintained an experimental nursery near the E. B. Dean mill at Eastside where he grew mostly Douglas-fir seedlings for out-planting.

Railroads were part of the Smith-Powers business empire. It is said that when Powers came to Oregon he brought with him the steel rails that had been used in his Minnesota operation. In addition to the E. B. Dean Company rail operations at Cunningham Creek, Smith and Powers acquired two engines and track from the Coos Bay Lumber and Coal Company's line (Larson Timber Company) in Beaver Hill. This company had built a short-line railroad to reach a potential coal prospect beneath their timber land. The coal prospect did not work out and the railroad went to Smith and Powers.

The enterprising pair also ran numerous logging operations around the Coos Bay area and built several different short-line railroads to serve them. In 1909, they operated four different logging railroads close to the bay, and in 1911 they had eight logging camps going:

- Camp No. 1 on Cunningham Creek
- Camp No. 2 on Isthmus Slough
- Camp No. 3 on North Coos River
- Camp No. 4 on South Inlet (at the mouth of Winchester Creek)
- Camps No. 5, No. 6, and No. 7 on Isthmus Slough
In September 1911 Camp No. 8 was opened at the head

A Bucyrus steamshovel building a siding for the Eden Ridge line of the Smith-Powers Logging Company, circa 1918. Coos Historical and Maritime Museum Box H20-980-233

of navigation on the South Fork of the Coos River, where a railroad 7,500 feet in length was built into the woods. Since the timber at this camp was more than 1,000 feet above the river, a rail incline averaging 20 percent grade was built to reach the harvest areas. At the head of Isthmus Slough some nine miles south of the old coal mining town of Henryville the company built a rail line into Camp No. 2, which ran for three miles on a trestle along the east side of the slough before it reached solid ground and continued into Smith's ownership near Greenacres. Smith had some 150 million board feet of timber in this area and he needed it for his mill.

Camps No. 5 and No. 6 were on the opposite side of Isthmus Slough about two miles southwest of Henryville. Logs from these camps were dumped into South Slough at the same site as those logs from Camp No. 2. Camp No. 7 was a couple of miles east of Coos City on the east side of the Slough with a separate rail line accessing that timber. Once the logs were dumped into Isthmus Slough, they were placed in a raft for storage and later towed to the mill.

Camp No. 3 was on Hodges Creek, a tributary of the North Fork of the Coos River, about six miles above

Albert Henry Powers, circa 1915. *From Early Coos County Loggers* by Curt Beckham

Smith-Powers Logging Company camp staff at Eden Ridge, circa 1936, Bandon Historical Museum 220 28371

A loading platform on Eden Ridge line with switchback, circa 1915, University of Washington Special Collections, Clark Kinsey Collection 806

Allegany. Logs were dumped into the river at the confluence for a river drive to Allegany where they were collected into rafts for the long tow to the mill.

Camp No. 4 was located three miles above the head of South Inlet, a tributary slough to the lower Coos Bay. A three-mile rail line was built to reach Smith's prime Port Orford Cedar and Sitka Spruce timber growing in that basin. Logs were dumped into the headwaters of South Slough, assembled into rafts and towed to the mill. Since the tow from Camp No. 4 to the mill had to pass the inlet to Coos Bay from the Pacific Ocean, great care had to be exercised in stormy weather.

When the timber around the Coos Bay area became depleted, the Smith-Powers Logging Company built a nineteen-mile rail line from Myrtle Point to Powers. The line connected with the old Coos Bay, Roseburg and Eastern Rail Road and Navigation Company mainline running from Myrtle Point to Marshfield. By then the CBR&ERR&N had sold its operations to the Southern Pacific Company. Construction of the new railroad from Myrtle Point began in 1912. One of the first steps involved Captain Olson and the C. A. Smith steamship *Nann Smith* (named for one of Smith's daughters). Olson turned command of the *Nann Smith* over to his first mate and immediately traveled to the Atlantic coast, where he took command of the *Adeline Smith* (named for another of Smith's daughters), which was loaded with steel rails for the Myrtle Point-Powers line. Captain Olson sailed her safely around Cape Horn and up the Pacific Coast to Coos Bay.

The first logs to come out over the new railroad came from a spur built up Baker Creek to access Smith's property in 1914. Smith also owned a massive amount of fine-grained timber on the hills to the south and west of the new town of Powers, Oregon. Three more spurs were needed; one up the South Fork of the Coquille River, one up Salmon Creek, and a final one up Eden Ridge.

As Al Powers was building Smith's railroads up the south fork of the Coquille River, into the Salmon Creek drainage, and on to the Eden Ridge system, additional plans were being made to tunnel into the Sixes River watershed from the Salmon Creek line. This section was never built. Instead a 6,000-foot incline was built with the terminus just a few feet from the Curry County line.

One of the markets tapped by the Smith-Powers Logging Company was for Port Orford Cedar (locally known as White Cedar or POC). The name is derived from the small coastal town of Port Orford on the southern Oregon coast about forty miles south of Coos Bay.

POC is relatively rare, growing only in mixed conifer stands along the coasts of southern Oregon and northern California, and is prized for its remarkable machining properties and rot resistance. It is also esteemed by Japanese home builders and for Japanese temples as it belongs to the same genus as the Emperor Cedar in Japan, making it quite valuable. Probably the best-known use of POC in the first half of the twentieth century was in battery separators; its unique oils made the wood resistant to the battery acids. POC also worked well for railroad ties and is remarkably long-lived when in contact with seawater, so was used for ship decking, marine piling, and the superstructures of smaller boats. In 1883, the Oregon Southern Improvement Company (a predecessor company of Menasha Corporation of Wisconsin) used POC for the piling to support a large sawmill on the tide flats of Empire City, Oregon. Forty years later, Louis J. Simpson observed, "Before we purchased the mill, we made a very careful examination of the foundation and found it after all these years to be in a perfect state of preservation. The remarkable preservation of this foundation is a source of wonder to all who see it and we never lose an opportunity to point it out to visitors to the mill."

In addition, several large box and broom handle plants were built around Coos County to utilize POC's unique properties. The large land holdings of C. A. Smith around Powers, Oregon, held a very large inventory of this valuable timber. With the demand for POC rising, the company was sitting on a veritable "green gold mine."

In 1915, a problem arose with the Southern Pacific line running between Myrtle Point and Coos Bay. The SP, which recently had completed its rail line from Eugene into Marshfield, increased the tariff on the Myrtle Point-Marshfield portion, resulting in a negative impact on Smith's mill at Isthmus Slough. Smith was incensed by the increase and turned to the county for a franchise to

Work crew building the Smith-Powers rail line between Myrtle Point and Powers, circa 1913. Oregon Historical Society

As with most other railroad loggers of the time, the Smith-Powers Logging Company used trestles wherever possible. It was much cheaper than digging the grade with steamshovels and allowed straighter track than would be possible following the contours of the land. University of Washington Special Collections, Clark Kinsey Collection 773

build a parallel line along the county road between the two communities.

Coos County granted the permit and Smith immediately began construction. His bluff worked. The SP and Smith entered into a more amicable agreement to jointly operate the existing line.

An article carried on the internet (http://www. brian894x4.com/ georgiaPacificCoosBayRR/html) does an excellent job of summarizing some of the general operations of the Smith-Powers operation.

According to the site:

Before the 1919, Smith-Powers Logging Company had 11 company camps, operating 65 steam donkeys, plus contracted work out to another four. The company had been the first to experiment with electric logging and became one of the largest purchasers of early diesel donkeys. They still however, were buying new steam donkeys as they had more pull for handling the large logs on Eden Ridge. During the early days, the fleets of lokies were transporting about 1.5-2 million feet of logs to the mill on two shifts during each work day. In 1929 the first of the new style of saddle tankers was ordered, and one or two of these then handled 100-120 car log trains to McCormac spur using the newer 56-64 foot cars. During the late 1930s the tide of mechanization and labor was changing. An experiment as to converting over to truck haul in 1938 proved more expensive, and sub-contracting labor failed also. In 1940 the company bucked the trend, and bought their own trucks, and hired hundreds of persons for woods work.

Not to lose sight of benefit of truck hauling, reloads were established. Two ponds were operated at Powers, another was built at Johnson (east of Coquille) and the one at Coquille was expanded over time to become the world's largest during the 1950s. The two ponds at Powers handled logs from Eden Ridge, Yellow Creek and Salmon Creek. The Johnson pond was built to handle oversized trucks operating on company maintained dirt roads which paralleled Highway 42. The Coquille pond came in the purchase of the Smith Wood Products firm in 1944 and handled the logs from Fairview and other areas of the

Cunningham district.

It was envisioned in the 1920s to extend the Cunningham railroad over the Coos Bay Military Wagon Road to a place on the upper Coos River where logs could be floated to the mill. Although promises had been made by the S. P. to extend track beyond Myrtle Point to Roseburg, equally ambitious were the efforts by the Coos Bay Lumber Company to extend their logging track eastward into Douglas County for a connection with the Southern Pacific at Cow Creek.

Today, three of the old Coos Bay Lumber Company locomotives have been preserved—in Cottage Grove is the Alco 2-8-2t No. 10; No. 11 is in San Diego at the Pacific Southwest Railway Museum; and No. 104 is in Coos Bay at the Railroad Museum. Technical information about the individual locomotives operated by the Smith-Powers Logging Company and photographs can be found in an appendix to this book.

BUILDING THE MYRTLE POINT TO POWERS LINE

As mentioned earlier, by 1912, Smith needed access to his 27,000 acres of timberland lying west of the South Fork of the Coquille River, and he and Al Powers figured out how to build the railroad they needed. It would connect the Wagner Ranch (now the town of Powers, Oregon) with the CBR&ERR&N rail line at Myrtle Point—a distance of nineteen miles.

The contract was let to Willet and Burr with Superintendent Ross in charge of operations, but before the line was completed, Powers took over the construction from the contractor. As the work progressed, contracts to feed the large crew of men were awarded and tent cookhouses appeared along the construction route.

EDEN RIDGE AND SALMON CREEK LINES

In 1918 as the rail line moved farther west from the small but growing town of Powers, significantly steeper terrain was encountered. The Salmon Creek line was projected to cover fifteen miles with a maximum grade of 1.65 percent and only twelve degrees of curvature in the layout. However there proved to be seven miles of very difficult terrain as the railroad progressed up the canyon. Solid rock faces had to be blasted away before the road

could continue. Powers was quoted as saying if the road bed stays in place after the dynamite blast, it would hold the log train. Several tunnels were built on this line as a judgment call to hold costs down. As an example, tunnel No. 1 was twenty-one-and-a-half feet high and provided fourteen-and-a-half feet of clearance over the tracks. It was 220 feet in length. There were also five switchbacks needed to gain the ridgeline between Salmon Creek and the Sixes River drainage to the west. Four billion board feet of high-quality Douglas fir and Port Orford Cedar was reported to be accessible from this line.

The Eden Ridge line was equally challenging. It was also estimated to be fifteen miles in length, with five switchbacks and a couple of inclines. There was an estimated seven billion board feet of fine quality timber in this area. The Eden Ridge line left the town of Powers (elevation 285 feet above sea level) and climbed to 3,400 feet before reaching the plateau on top, gaining more than a half mile of elevation over just fifteen miles. In places the line had to be blasted out of solid sandstone to keep the road on grade. It cost a good deal of money in those days to build these lines. For example, a four-mile long spur built from the 1,400 foot elevation mark cost $50,000 per mile.

Al Powers employed several techniques to deal with the rugged topography of the coastal mountains. He built tunnels where he had no other alternatives—tunneling

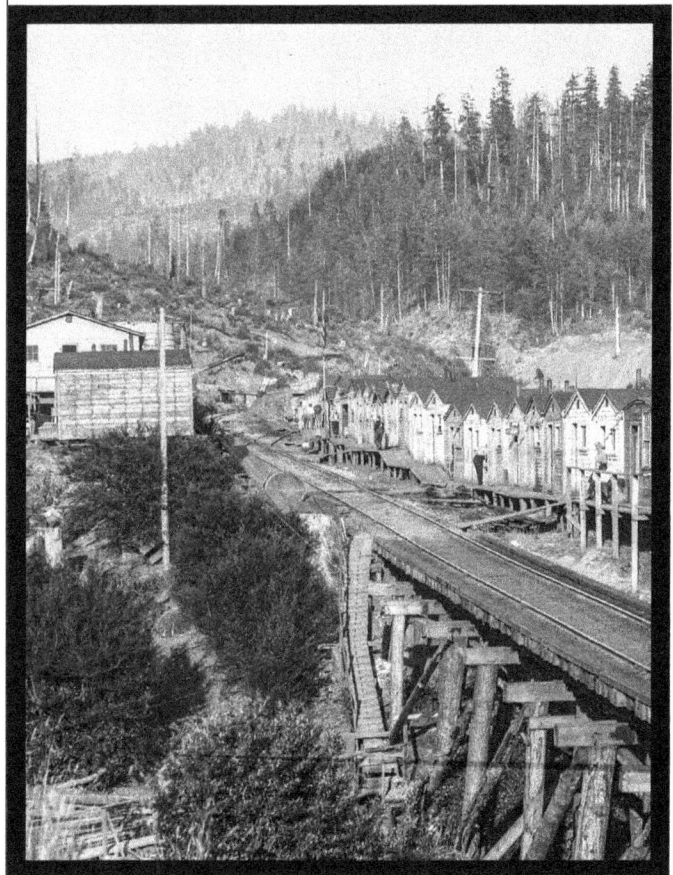

was expensive and dangerous. He used inclines as the least expensive method to gain elevation, but also used switchbacks—generally built in conjunction with low trestles. Confronted with steep terrain and deep draws, Powers maintained a survey crew to locate the best route to lay in the grade.

As with all high-lead logging operations in the steep country of Coos County, a strategically located spar tree had to be found and the top removed in order to "rig" it for use. The spar trees were prepared for the Smith-Powers Logging Company by a Swede named William Stromberg. Everyone knew him as "High Lead Bill." The spar trees in the Powers area were often 200 feet tall. High Lead Bill would usually use an axe to chop a girdle or wide notch around the circumference of the tree at the spot where the top of the spar tree was needed, close to the top, where the tree's diameter was about twenty-two inches. He would then fill the slot with enough blasting powder to break the tree at the notch; when it was detonated, the top of the tree would blow off. Another technique was to ring the tree at the location where the top of the spar was needed with sticks of dynamite held firmly in place with rope, like a string of sausages. The fuse to set off the dynamite was usually ten feet in length with a bum rate of one foot per minute. A safety line was attached to the blasting cap high in the tree. If for some reason High Lead Bill got delayed in his descent, the line was pulled and the charge nullified.

There are conflicting stories about how Al Powers treated his loggers. Some writers described a tough-minded, straight-talking woods boss, while others discussed how well the Smith-Powers company treated their men. Since no one is alive today to testily one way or the other, editorializing is left up to the particular persuasion of the writer. Nonetheless, when the Industrial Workers of the World (IWW) came on the scene, very little labor unrest was experienced in the Smith- Powers Logging Company—a tribute to their leadership. However, the company did finally comply with the "Wobblies'" demands for clean sheets in the bunk houses every Saturday, cleaning and de-lousing of the bunkhouses once a week, and the use of china plates in the cook house. While the living conditions in the logging camps were improving, probably the greatest result of the union's

The *Pacific* was built in 1910 by the Kruse and Banks firm of North Bend, Oregon, specifically for Al Powers. It was forty feet long and was used by Powers to visit the logging camps around Coos Bay. Coos Art Museum 1295

involvement was to focus attention on safety.

As operations expanded and living conditions for the loggers improved the logging camps became quite comfortable, with many accommodating not only loggers but their families as well.

While Al Powers is rightly given credit for keeping Smith's mills well supplied with logs, the daily chores fell to the camp foremen who worked for the Smith-Powers company. In 1918, those men were:

- Camp 1 William Garrett
- Camp 2 Charles Hamlin
- Camp 3 D. Brown
- Camp 4 A. W. Marshall
- Camp 5 James Pybum
- Camp 6 Ed McKeown
- Camp 7 Gene Grant
- Camp 8 Frank Carey

Smith-Powers had assembled a massive amount of logging and railroad equipment to tackle the job of removing the 12-13 billion board feet of timber from Eden Ridge and Salmon Creek:

- Three 125-ton Baldwin locomotives for the main rail line to Coos Bay
- One 75-ton Heisler locomotive
- One 40-ton Climax locomotive
- Three 42-ton Shay locomotives
- Two 32-ton Shay locomotives
- 204 railroad log cars
- Fifteen Willamette donkeys and forty-five smaller donkeys

A little known fact about the Smith-Powers logging camps in the Powers area was that during the summer and fall of 1918, the company employed 182 soldiers from the Spruce Production Division (see more about this effort later in the book). The soldiers were apportioned to the various logging camps and worked alongside the civilian loggers.

The Ranger was a forty-four-foot gasoline powered tug used to tow log rafts from shallow draft regions around the bay. According to notes of Victor West, her last enrollment papers in July 1951 indicated "vessel dismantled". Coos Art Museum 598

Their pay was the same as the regular loggers. When the Armistice was signed, these soldier-loggers returned home to along with their counterparts who were logging in the Beaver Slough area. Undoubtedly some returned to the woods after they "mustered out" of the army.

In addition to the large mill complex that Smith operated at the mouth of Isthmus Slough and the extensive rail and logging camps worked throughout Coos County, the company also maintained a fleet of small boats for use on Coos Bay. In total Smith and Powers operated several small gas-powered boats ranging from 5-60 horsepower. Among the boats were the *Mayflower, Teddy Bear, Mable H., Wolf II, Mad Hen, Dixie,* and *Leader.*

The *General II* was twenty-nine feet long with a 4' 3" beam and a gas motor that generated twenty-nine horsepower. It was long and thin. The boat was purchased by Powers for the purpose of traveling to each logging camp operating with access to the bay. It was reported to be the fastest speedboat on the Pacific coast. Apparently Powers liked the speed, but each time he ventured out in the *General II*, he returned drenched with salt spray. As a consequence, during foul weather Powers started using the *Pacific* which had a covered cabin, but could only make eighteen miles per hour. Powers was cited several times for violating the Port speed law of six miles per hour while passing the Marshfield boat moorage.

Smith's timber empire in Oregon began to crumble in 1914. His insatiable appetite for growth had caused him to leverage the company assets to the limit. When the lumber

A view of Camp No. 6 at Powers from part way up the incline. University of Washington Special Collections, Clark Kinsey Collection 4065

market crashed after World War I, bond underwriters forced the company and all of its subsidiaries into an involuntary reorganization in 1919. Smith's son Vernon was appointed by the court as manager of the operation and Al Power's son Fred continued to manage the logging operation. The creditors essentially allowed the business of the company to continue uninterrupted. C. A. Smith retained an interest in the operation and was an advisor to his son, even after moving to California with his wife Johanna.

The mill continued to run under the Coos Bay Lumber

California Lumber Company locomotive. Coos Historical and Maritime Museum, Jack Slattery Collection 992-8-0263

George Chaney Logging Company at Glen Aiken Creek, circa 1927. Shay No. 1 was fueled by diesel oil. Coos Historical and Maritime Museum, Jack Slattery Collection 992-8-0197

Company name until 1922, when it was officially reorganized as the Pacific States Lumber Company. In 1928, C. E. Dant of the Dant and Russell Company in Portland and E. E. Adelsperger, president of the Western White Cedar Company, purchased the Salmon Creek rail line and the 23,000 acres of timberland tributary to the railroad. The property reportedly had 200 million board feet of Port Orford Cedar and 900 million board feet of Douglas fir timber remaining. Even after the sale, the Coos Bay Lumber Company had considerable timber assets with which to supply its mill. The company continued to operate under the business name of Coos Bay Lumber Company until it was sold to Georgia Pacific in 1956.

On December 9, 1925, Charles Axel Smith died of cancer in Berkeley, California. Al Powers left the company when it was reorganized. He died in an automobile crash on January 2, 1930, in Indio, California.

Smith's main railroad lasted longer than almost any other in the region. Log cars from the Eden Ridge and Salmon Creek spurs were brought to Powers, where they began a forty-five- mile trek to Smith's big mill at the head of Isthmus Slough.

The speed on the mainline track was ten miles per hour—tops. The last log train pulled out of Powers station destined for the McCormac log dump on Isthmus Slough on June 16, 1972, long after the other rail lines had faded into history. The tracks from Myrtle Point to Powers were pulled up and shipped to Bangkok, Thailand, in 1973.

CALIFORNIA LUMBER COMPANY

The California Lumber Company, organized in early 1888, purchased property about a mile south of the old Simpson mill in North Bend. It became known as the Porter property (named after the major stockholder of the company) and a sawmill the company built at that location became known as the Porter

Mill. Lumber for its construction was supplied by the E. B. Dean Company mill at Isthmus Slough. The Porter mill could handle logs up to fifty feet in length, and the site included a large store and houses built for the workmen. The first logs were cut in October 1888.

Between 1890 and 1902, California Lumber had two and a half miles of railroad track at Sumner, Oregon, on which the company ran a thirty-one-ton Baldwin locomotive, and also logged at other locations on the Coos River. The Simpson Lumber Company purchased the California Lumber Company's assets in November 1902".

CHANEY LOGGING COMPANY

In 1923 George Chaney took a logging contract on property owned by the Coos Bay Lumber Company in the Glenn Aiken Creek watershed just south of Coquille. He had been logging in the area since about 1910 and was quite familiar with the timber. Since considerable Bureau of Land Management timberland surrounded this property, Chaney figured he could continue to log in the basin indefinitely. He therefore built a railroad with excess ballast and grade of the quality that rivaled that of the Southern Pacific. In fact the first two miles of the current Glenn Aiken county road was later built along this same grade. In addition to the ballast used on the grade, there were two ninety-foot-high trestles built—one about three quarters of a mile up the current county road and another at the very end. While one can imagine the trestle while traveling the county road, there is no evidence of it today.

Chaney had an unusual method of logging. He made a portable yarder out of a large steam donkey placed on a flatcar pulled by a locomotive. The yarder also had a large boom that gave it a "portable spar." A siding would be built off the main rail line, the yarder pulled onto the siding, the spar pole raised, and guy-lines secured. The old timers called these machines "tower skidders."

The Great Depression wreaked havoc on the Chaney logging operation. By the early 1930s, the company's railroad logging operation in Glenn Aiken Creek was finished.

CODY LUMBER COMPANY

The Cody Lumber Company partners, just like Charles Axel Smith, were Minnesota timbermen. With that region's pine forests fast becoming depleted around the turn of the century, they sought additional timber tracts in Oregon and Washington. In the February 7, 1905, edition of the Coquille City Herald it was reported that Mr. L. J. Cody and Addis of Duluth, Minnesota, had arrived in Coquille and were visiting timberlands in the Lampa Creek area along with Colonel William Coach. They announced that they planned to build a large sawmill on the Coquille River near Bandon, Oregon, and would begin logging the 5,000 acres they owned adjacent to the creek. The local paper reported the company's inventory on the land was in excess of 400 million board feet. The *Timberman* magazine in June

Cody Logging Company timber fallers at Lampa Creek, circa 1908. Coos Historical and Maritime Museum, Jack Slattery Collection 992-8-0429

1905 reported that the Capital stock of Cody Lumber Company was $100,000; L. J. Cody, M. J. McKenna, and Walter Sinclair were listed as incorporators.

On August 27, 1909, the Coos Bay Harbor newspaper reported that the Cody mill at Bandon was completely destroyed by fire, but indicated that the company was still financially strong, with the principal owners being Colonel C. E. Coach of Chicago, George W. Moore of Michigan, and J. L. Cody and Colonel R. H. Rosa of Bandon. Moore and Coach apparently had the largest interest in the mill. The mill was rebuilt and started back up on May 16, 1910. In July 1910 issue of Timberman magazine it was reported that the mill was known as the George W. Moore and Lumber Company. The operation eventually became known as the Moore Mill and Lumber Company. They had separate logging and railroad operations at Leneve, Oregon.

The North Bend locomotive, originally owned by Simpson, and later by his contractors McDonald and Vaughn, it was sold to Cody Logging (it is seen here at the Cody Camp at Lampa Creek), then went to the Conlogue logging operation at Leneve. From there it sat out on a dock on the Coquille River until being cut up for scrap in World War II. Coos Art Museum

Cody Lumber Company incline at Lampa Creek. Coos Htorical and Maritime Museum, Jack Slattery Collection 992 -8 -0530

CODY LUMBER COMPANY

The Cody Mill at Bandon, Oregon. Bandon Historical Museum

Cody Logging Camp at Lampa Creek, Coos County, Oregon. Coquile Valley Museum 2006-25-026

Conlogue logging operation, Lampa Creek camp, with a Willamette "wide face" donkey.
Coos Historical and Maritime Museum,
Jack Slattery Collection
992-8-0527

Conlogue logging operation at Lampa Creek in 1910. Coos Historical and Maritime Museum, Jack Slattery Collection 992-8-0528

CONLOGUE LOGGING COMPANY

In 1928, William P. McKenna, Jack P. Dillon, and John Thomas Conlogue (bom October 23,1875) of Bandon, Oregon, purchased 1,040 acres of timberland in the South Slough area from the Southwestern Oregon Company. It contained 40 million board feet of spruce and Port Orford Cedar. In January 1928 M. J. McKenna (president), John T. Conlogue (vice president), and William McKenna (treasurer) were listed as incorporators of Conlogue Logging Company with capital stock of $100,000.

Around 1928 Conlogue Logging built a railroad up Winchester Creek at the head of South Slough. The company moved its equipment and camp from the town of Leneve on the Coquille River, where the crew had been logging for George Moore. At Leneve, they built a logging railroad to the ridge dividing the Coquille River watershed and South Slough. Conlogue located his camp at South Slough at the same spot as the Smith-Powers Logging Company some years before. The Conlogues were related to the McKenna family, and in partnership logged in the South Slough area until the Great Depression.

Three logging/mill companies were interconnected at this time: Cody Lumber (subscribers: L. J. Cody, M. J. McKenna, and Walter Sinclair) incorporated on May 5, 1905; Conlogue Logging; and George W. Moore Lumber (subscribers: George W. Moore, L. J. Cody, M. J. McKenna, and C. R. Moore) incorporated on January 4, 1910. Moore Lumber was absorbed into the Moore Mill and Lumber Company on April 18, 1916.

The J. F. Dunham logging crew and cook house in Coos County in 1872. Coos Historical and Maritime Museum, Jack Slattery Collection 992-8-0407

The J. F. Dunham logging operation on Isthmus Slough using the Isabella. Judd Mills is the engineer, circa 1880. Coos County Logging Museum

J. F. DUNHAM

Dunham is a name connected with William Utter and the Isthmus Transit Railroad. J. F. Dunham was sent to San Francisco by Utter in 1874 to purchase the steam locomotive Isabella to carry coal from Litter's Carbondale coal mine at Coaledo over Utter's rail line at Isthmus Slough. When the coal prospect failed, Dunham purchased the Isabella and used her to haul logs from the Coaledo area. He never built a rail line himself.

Dunham also owned and operated a sawmill on the west side of Isthmus Slough just below the current community of Millington. The rail line was used to transport logs to Isthmus Slough, where they were dumped into the water and towed in rafts to his mill. The mill had the capacity of cutting some 27,000 board feet per day in 1875. The *Coos Bay News* on June 30, 1875 reported that "The schooner *C.W. Merithew* loaded at Utter City last week took 150 tons of coal, two cords of match wood, and 5,500 feet of flooring from Dunham's mill."

With the cargo, she drew only 8' 9" of water. This shipment of lumber was the first from the mill on the Isthmus."

Later that year, Dunham fell onto hard times and the sawmill was sold at a sheriffs sale. Adam Lobree, the purchaser, hauled the machinery away and installed it in his mill at Marshfield.

MCDONALD AND VAUGHN
COOS BAY LOGGING COMPANY

William "Bill" Vaughn came to Marshfield, Oregon, in 1900 after graduating from a Portland business college, and went to work for the Simpson Lumber Company. As his grandson Mike Vaughn of Coos Bay tells the story, Louis Simpson had asked the superintendent of the business college to send him the very best student to be an accounting clerk/administrative assistant for his company—fully expecting a female candidate. He must have been surprised when Bill Vaughn showed up on the steamer from Portland to handle the job.

As Vaughn worked over the Simpson Lumber Company books during the next few years, he began to realize his real passion lay in the logging end of the business. In 1900 Simpson had formed a partnership with three other men (King, Bradbury, and Noble), who called the resulting business the Coos Bay Logging Company. The group began logging some of the Simpson Lumber Company timberlands at Daniels Creek. Simpson formed the Daniels Creek Railroad Company in 1898 for the purpose of hauling logs from that drainage. The logging partnership did not last long and Louis Simpson reorganized the rail company under the new name of the Blue Ridge Rail Road and Navigation Company—an organization in which Bill Vaughn would play an integral part.

In 1907, Vaughn and Jack McDonald picked up the pieces of the original Coos Bay Logging Company and began work as an independent logging contractor for Simpson. Louis Simpson was a quiet third partner in the logging venture, supplying most of the equipment. McDonald and Vaughn first used a Dolbeer steam donkey with a single spool as their main yarding machine. Logs were pulled along skid roads to the central landing site where the donkey was positioned. A horse was used to pull the cable back out for the next turn of logs. Whether factual or imaginary, most all who wrote about this operation claimed the horse was always white.

For the next several years, McDonald and Vaughn logged the side slopes of Daniels Creek. The logs from the operation were hauled by train to the log dump at the junction of Coos River. The engine they used, called the North Bend, was a 4-4-0 (see appendix for definition) locomotive built by Danforth and Cooke.

At the head of Daniels Creek lies a flat-topped marine terrace called Blue Ridge, where Simpson owned some 10,000 acres. This region had some of the very best timber in the area and Simpson needed access to it.

The big problem was getting a railroad from the floor of Daniels Creek up the steep side slope of Blue Ridge to

Timber fallers cutting high quality Douglas-fir timber, circa 1914. Coos Historical and Maritime Museum H-26 987-19.29

Blue Ridge timber logged by McDonald and Vaughn, circa 1914. Coos Historical and Maritime Museum, Jack Slattery Collection 992-8-04-71

the top. McDonald and Vaughn solved it by building a long incline traversing the westerly side of the ridge. The incline was the longest in the region, stretching for 8,500 feet with an average grade of 17 percent. A specially designed "lowering steam donkey" named the Coos King was used for the long pull. Once at the top of the ridge, the company built spurs to access Simpson's timber.

One of the major problems facing the Daniels Creek and Blue Ridge operations was getting equipment and supplies to the logging camps. There were no roads or rail lines from Marshfield at that time, and all material had to be brought to the junction of Daniels Creek and the Coos River on a barge. Railroad ties, track, and even the heavy locomotives had to be transported up the Coos River, off-loaded onto a rail spur, and the line built from there. In the beginning, when Louis Simpson first built the rail line up Daniels Creek the steam pile driver was first on the scene. It began by driving piling to build a low trestle upon which the cross beams were attached and eventually the rails. The locomotive would then be off-loaded from the barge and the process continued as Simpson moved farther up the valley floor.

Mike Vaughn relayed another interesting story about his grandfather's logging company. Recreation at the logging camps was limited to playing cards or telling stories. But the McDonald and Vaughn group decided to add one more dimension to their relaxing time—baseball. They formed a team in the woods, the Blue Ridge Tigers. This group soon earned a reputation for hard fighting, heavy drinking, and generally enjoying the pleasures attendant to the "skid row" area of Marshfield/North Bend. They were always looking for competition of any sort, battling tough local teams like the Powers Cubs representing the Smith-Powers Logging Company at Eden Ridge. The games could get pretty fierce. The Cubs carried two tame black bears with them just in case they needed a little friendly advantage.

Jack McDonald died in 1921 and the ownership consolidated into Vaughn, Simpson, and Winsor. After McDonald died, Vaughn moved the logging operation

MCDONALD AND VAUGHN—COOS BAY LOGGING COMPANY

The McDonald and Vaughn Logging Company (Coos Bay Logging Company) used Shay locomotive No. 765 along the plateau of Blue Ridge, circa 1903. Coos Historical and Maritime Museum, Jack Slattery Collection 992 -8 -0484

The Coos King donkey used to lower loaded log cars down the face of Blue Ridge to the waiting locomotive in the valley below. The Coos King was built by the Willamette Iron and Steel Company specifically for the very long incline at Blue Ridge, Coos Historical and Maritime Museum, Jack Slattery Collection 992 -8 -0510

The McDonald and Vaughn Logging Company (Coos Bay Logging Company) used Shay locomotive No. 765 along the plateau of Blue Ridge, circa 1903. Coos Historical and Maritime Museum, Jack Slattery Collection 992 -8 -0484

McDonald and Vaughn unloading supplies from a barge at the mouth of Daniels Creek. Coos Historical and Maritime Museum, Jack Slattery Collection 992-8-0487.

Baseball was a magnet for all. Here the McDonald and Vaughn "family" are enjoying a trip on the flatcar on the Coos River. Jack McDonald is sitting on locomotive step. Coos Historical and Maritime Museum, Jack Slattery Collection 992-8-0481

The infamous Blue Ridge Tigers of the McDonald and Vaughn Logging Company. Coos Historical and Maritime Museum Box 28 988-P3B

Powers Baseball Team. Coos Historical and Maritime Museum 992-8-1991

to the south end of Blue Ridge a few miles east of Sumner and built a new rail line up Seelander Creek. The company logged in this region for several more years. They also logged for a brief time at Green Acres, Oregon.

In 1936 the McKinley-Fairview fire burned through much of Blue Ridge especially in T. 27 S., R. 12 W., leaving much of the area logged by McDonald and Vaughn denuded of its regrowth. The fire report indicates that the conflagration, started by a smoker on September 25, 1936, burned a total of 22,660 acres. It was not declared "out" by the Oregon State Forestry Department until November 5, 1936.

In 1925, Bill Vaughn and Ben R. Chandler bought out the interests of Simpson and Winsor and took over the old Simpson mill from Stout Lumber, where Vaughn had started his career twenty-five years earlier.

A final note is worthy of mention. Not only was Bill Vaughn creative in his logging endeavors, he also had an interest in reforestation—long before any laws were on the books that required replanting or re-seeding after logging. Vaughn had his own nursery from which trees were planted on land suitable for timber production.

NOBLE LOGGING COMPANY

One of the first railroad loggers in Coos County, a man by the name of Noble, left very little information about his operation. Noble used a Hinkley locomotive that first saw Work at Flanagan's and Mann's Libby Coal Mine, before Noble bought it and used it to haul logs out of Blossom Gulch near Marshfield.

PACIFIC WHITE CEDAR COMPANY

With Port Orford Cedar (POC or "white cedar" as it is locally known) being one of the more valuable species of trees growing in Coos County, it seems logical that someone would take up its name for a company. In fact, there were numerous small sawmills scattered around the county that cut POC. The Evans Product company made an exceptionally fine business out of making POC rotary veneer for battery separators. And young Carroll Smith used the scrap Port Orford Cedar from his father's mill to make wooden window blinds for the market in the east.

McDonald and Vaughn logging on Blue Ridge. Note the "log cribbing" under the track. This technique was good enough as long as the track remained relatively level and the road held together for the time needed to finish the logging. Holding logging costs down was the sign of a successful logger. Coos Historical and Maritime Museum, Jack Slattery Collection 992-8-0485

Train accident at the Vaughn and Simpson Logging operation at Seelander Creek, 1922. Coos Historical and Maritime Museum, Jack Slattery Collection 992-8-0468

The Noble Logging Company's Hinkley engine, manufactured by the Fulton Iron Works San Francisco, California, in October 1872. Coos Historical and Maritime Museum, Jack Slattery Collection 992-8-0183

George Pike logging operation at Sevenmile Slough, 1902. Note the "cheese blocks" on the landing skids designed to hold the logs in place before being rolled onto the rail trucks. The reach between the rail trucks can also be seen. Coos Historical and Maritime Museum Box 33 989J100A

The Prosper Mill Company logging camp at Sevenmile Slough showing the cook house and cabins for the loggers along with the company train and modified Dolbeer donkey, circa 1912. Coos Historical and Maritime Museum, Jack Slattery Collection 992-8-0434

PIKE LOGGING

George Pike ran a very successful bull team operation in the Sevenmile Slough area, and also had a narrow gauge railroad.

PROSPER MILL COMPANY

The Prosper Mill Company was best known for the mill Adam Pershbaker built at the town of Prosper in the mid 1880s. The original mill was designed to cut wide dimension (24 inch-36 inch width) Port Orford Cedar lumber. By 1902, when Pershbaker sold the mill, it was cutting around four million board feet per year.

The peak growth and development of Prosper occurred between 1910 and 1920. In addition to the rugged area's largest elementary school, which accommodated grades 1-12, the town had a post office, general store, grocery store, two sawmills, a shipyard, salmon cannery, and several smaller salmon salting and pickling operations. The Prosper Mill Company also owned timberland and a logging railroad at Sevenmile Slough located on the north side of the Coquille River. In August 1929, the Prosper Mill Company sawmill was destroyed by fire.

RANDOLPH LUMBER COMPANY

In 1911 the Randolph Lumber Company operated a large sawmill at the town of Randolph, upstream from Bandon on the Coquille River. The mill was built by Carman and Crities in 1901. The company's main railroad line, located on Bear Creek, stretched some seven miles from Parkersburg on the Coquille River up Bear Creek to a large tract of timberland (around 4,000 acres). The logs from this

The Prosper Mill Company logging operation at Camp No. 5 at Sevenmile Slough, circa 1900. From left, Allen Leneve, Elmer McCue, Frank Carlson, and Charlie McCue. Coos Historical and Maritime Museum, Jack Slattery Collection 992-8-0433

The Prosper Mill Company logging operation at Sevenmile Slough in 1914. Note the bucking saw used to cut the firewood to fuel the steam donkey's boiler. Coos Historical and Maritime Museum, Jack Slattery Collection 992-8-0436

The Ralph Hewitt Rosa log hauling operation near Bandon, Oregon, circa 1900. Adam Pershberger is shown standing to the right of the planked road with Rosa to his left, Coos Historical and Maritime Museum, Jack Slattery Collection 982-8-1903

operation were loaded on rail cars for transportation to the Coquille River at Parkersburg, where they were dumped into the river, formed into rafts, and towed by a tugboat to the mill at Randolph.

There was reported to be an additional 500 million board feet of fine quality Douglas-fir timber within easy reach of the Bear Creek line. The company had planned to extend its railroad farther south within the drainage to tap large tracts of timber owned by other companies. The Seeley and Anderson Company did much of the contract logging for Randolph Lumber Company.

The company also operated in the Bill's Creek drainage east of Bandon, had a rail line in the Sevenmile Slough area, and ran another spur line off the main railroad built by Cody Lumber Company at Lampa Creek.

Randolph Lumber owned two Shay locomotives: No. 1 Shay-2 Lima #2518—rated at 42 tons, built May 1, 1912; No. 2 Shay-2 Lima #2603—rated 42 tons, built January 24, 1912.

Some time before November 25, 1912, the Randolph Lumber Company sold their logging operations and railroad to Seeley and Anderson. In 1911, the mill operations were sold to the Alfred Johnson Lumber Company (E. E. Johnson, President) who also owned interest in the Seeley and Anderson operation. Two years later, the mill burned to the ground.

RALPH HEWITT ROSA

In 1904 Ralph Hewitt Rosa of Bandon operated a white cedar portable sawmill and constructed a two-mile tram road using 6 inch by 6 inch stringers for rails. The stringers were capped with strap iron upon which he operated a rod locomotive. The operation continued for about six years. His mill cut only Port Orford Cedar for broom handles. Rosa was a member of the Oregon State legislature in 1876 representing Coos County as a Democrat.

ROMEO EDWARD SCRANTON

Scranton logged primarily in the Isthmus Slough area in the late 1880s and early 1890s. No written commentary was uncovered except for the following photographs about his operation.

Left: Ralph Hewitt Rosa

Below: R. E. Scranton
Coos Historical and Maritime Museum, Jack Slattery Collection 992-8-0402

Left: R. E. Scranton logging crew, 1889. Douglas County History Museum 3208

Below: R. E. Scranton logging operation at Isthmus Slough. This is another example of combining a bull team to skid the logs to a railhead. Scranton can be seen in the far background with the white beard, circa 1889.
Coos Historical and Maritime Museum, Jack Slattery Collection 992-8-0401

The men from the R.E. Scranton logging operation prepare to unload logs from rail cars on Isthmus Slough. the long pole being held by the man on the skidway—called a pike pole—is used to push the floating logs into a raft, circa 1889. Coos Historical and Maritime Museum, Jack Slattery Collection 992-8-0395.

This classic example of a home-bred iron mule lacks many of the refinements of the Shay, Heisler, or the Climax engines, but was a locomotive nonetheless. Undoubtedly this was the product of Scranton's ingenuity coupled with an excellent blacksmith. Regardless of its appearance, it indeed pulled a very credible load of logs to the dump from Scranton's logging camp further up in the hills. The logs have all been peeled with their ends "sniped" or beveled indicating they were first skidded to the rail siding by a team of oxen, circa 1889. Coos Historical Museum, Jack Slattery Collection 992-8-0396

SEELEY AND ANDERSON LUMBER COMPANY

The Seeley and Anderson Lumber Company had logging operations at Sevenmile Slough, Bear Creek, and Bill's Creek (a small tributary stream east of Bandon). The company was formed by O. J. Seeley, Nonda Anderson, and E. E. Johnson in October 1911. They were the primary contract loggers for the Prosper Mill Company between 1908 and 1914. Before then, they logged in the Beaver Hill area. In the early part of 1912, they purchased the railroad operations and locomotives from the Prosper Mill Company. The company was well known because of a spectacular and tragic trestle accident near Bill's Creek on November 25,1912. Three days later, the Coos Bay Harbor reported:

Monday morning at Fairy Creek six miles from Bandon, the most disastrous logging train wreck ever happening in Coos County occurred. Six of the seven men aboard the engine are now dead and the seventh is in the hospital badly scalded and burned. The train, a Shay engine with three heavily loaded flats, crashed through the 100 foot trestle and it took nearly 24 hours to recover the victims. Roland Anderson, burned and scalded, crawled from the wreckage to a camp ¼ mile away and gave the alarm. All others were pinioned beneath tons of logs and wreckage.

Another description was written years later by Dick Hancock (http:// bandonbythesea.com/news/crows.htm):

Just east of Bandon, there occurred one of the deadliest railroad logging accidents in the annals of logging history. In 1912, Seeley and Anderson were logging in the Bill's Creek area. They had constructed a logging railroad from there, about four miles to the Coquille River, using the latest model Shay locomotive as the motive power on the line. As anyone who has hiked in that area knows, there are several deep canyons that had to be crossed; one of them over 100 feet deep and 500 feet wide which had to be crossed with a timber trestle.

It was the inaugural run of the three car heavily loaded train that morning of November 25, 1912. Aboard the train were three crewmen and four passengers from the logging camp, including two who had been injured in woods accidents earlier who were going to town to the doctor.

The Seeley and Anderson Company trestle at Bill's Creek, early 1912. Coos Historical and Maritime Museum, Jack Slattery Collection 992-8-0532

The Seeley and Anderson railroad trestle collapsed November 25, 1912. Six men died as a result of the collapse, only one man survived—Roll Anderson. Coos Historical and Maritime Museum, Jack Slattery Collection 992-8-05035

A close-up view of the Seeley and Anderson Shay locomotive No. 2518 beneath the rubble f the trestle, 1912. Oregon History Society.

As the train headed out onto the high trestle, the engineer felt it "giving." Hastily applying the brakes, he transferred the weight of the heavy log cars forward, causing the framework of the trestle to collapse into the canyon, carrying train and men into the abyss.

The engineer had time only to cry, "Boys, we're gone," before the whole thing fell into a tangled heap of timbers and wreckage.

Three men were killed outright in the wreck. Three more died shortly after being pulled from the debris. One man managed, though badly injured, to crawl from the pile and go for help ...

The man who survived, Roll Anderson, was the brother of one of the owners of the company. The company was taken over by the Robert Dollar Lumber Company in 1914 through an involuntary receivership.

SIMPSON FAMILY COMPANIES

Captain Asa Meade Simpson, like many others from San Francisco, came to Coos Bay in search of opportunities in the timber industry (he was also interested in shipbuilding). He visited the area in 1850 and returned to start his business in 1853. Originally from Maine, Simpson quickly seized upon the opportunities at North Bend and built a sizable timber empire in the region that lasted some seventy years. While Simpson is probably best known for dominating the shipbuilding trade in the region, he also purchased thousands of acres of timberlands in Coos County, integrated his logging operations with a mill, and built ships to carry his lumber from Oregon to markets in San Francisco.

Simpson and Henry Heaton Luse were the first to grasp the opportunity of industrial sawmilling on Coos Bay. Luse built a mill at Empire City in 1853 and sold it to the Oregon Southern Improvement Company in 1883. Simpson completed his mill in 1855. It was located on the westerly shore of the eastern arm of Coos Bay at the toe of a peninsula that later became known as Simpson Heights (for more on Luse, see my earlier book *Seeing the Forest for the Trees*).

Captain Simpson died in 1915 after turning over his Coos Bay operations to his eldest son Louis J. Simpson in 1899. It seems as though the younger Simpson had more political aspirations than business focus. Shortly after the elder

Simpson died, the family timber empire was sold in 1916 to Phillip Buehner of Portland, Oregon.

To build his mill at North Bend, Asa Simpson purchased sawmill machinery previously used in Sutter's mill (where gold had been discovered in 1849) in the Sierra Nevada Mountain Range east of Sacramento, California. Simpson loaded the machinery aboard the sailing ship *Quandratus* in San Francisco, with his brother Louis P. Simpson aboard to supervise the shipment, and started north. Asa Simpson did not sail with the ship.

It appears that Luse and Asa Simpson had something of a race going to see which one would be the first to ship a lumber cargo across the Coos Bay bar. Luse's mill was almost finished when the *Quandratus* tried to cross the bar in a storm. The ship struck a reef and there it was held as waves pounded it. Several men lost

Portrait of Asa Meade Simpson, circa 1890s. Coos Historical and Maritime Museum H8 972-18C

Louis Jerome Simpson, circa 1920. Coos Historical and Maritime Museum 991-20.18

Simpson operation on Daniel's Creek—locomotive is the North Bend, circa 1899.
Coos Historical and Maritime Museum, Jack Slattery Collection 992-8-0497

The North Bend on a low trestle across the bottom land at Daniels Creek. Coos Historical and Maritime Museum H37-S2-989-P167

their lives in the incident, including Simpson's brother. The ship was finally blown free of the rocks and limped into Coos Bay, where it was met by a very dejected Asa Simpson. Since only a portion of the mill machinery survived the accident and the dejected Simpson had to purchase additional parts, Luse completed his sawmill first and probably won the wager with Simpson.

By the late 1880s the demand for logs could no longer be supplied from the hills immediately surrounding Coos Bay, and Simpson became one of the first to invest in significant timber holdings in outlying areas—primarily in the regions known as Daniels Creek and Blue Ridge. Not only had Simpson's mill grown by that time, but also the new Southern Oregon Company big mill at Empire and the E. B. Dean Company mill on Isthmus Slough were pushing log prices upward. Simpson's investments at Daniels Creek would prove to be very profitable and keep his operations supplied with logs.

Asa's son Louis J. Simpson first ventured into the railroad business when he built a line up Daniels Creek to haul logs from the "back country" of Coos County around 1898. The line was designed and built by Harry C. Noble, Hiram King, and Charles Bradbury, who formed the Coos Bay Logging Company and began logging the region for Simpson. Simpson incorporated the Coos Bay and Daniels Creek Rail Road first to shield this investment from any creditors he had in the mill operation. He then formed the Blue Ridge Rail Road and Navigation Company to handle the entire logging operation once the line reached the top of Blue Ridge.

The engine that Simpson first acquired for use on this specific rail line was a 4-4-0 locomotive built by the Danforth and Cooke Company. Simpson purchased the engine from the Union Pacific Rail Road Company where it had a shop number 1367. Simpson named it the North Bend, a name that followed the locomotive from owner to owner.

The Daniels Creek railroad was built to transport logs from various logging camps scattered along the creek. The line stopped at the junction of Daniels Creek and the Coos River, where a log dump was built. Several years later, the line was extended by McDonald and Vaughn to the top of Blue Ridge.

The first permanent logging camp that Simpson built

The North Bend locomotive brought to Coos County by the Simpson Lumber Company in 1898. Douglas County Historical Museum 4624

Simpson logging operation at Daniels Creek, 1889. A "towing donkey" was used to position the rail trucks under the log railway. The *North Bend* can be seen through the smoke and steam. A yarding donkey can be seen to the right of center in the photo with cable lying in the skid road.
Coos Historical and Maritime Museum, Jack Slattery Collection 992-8-0506

The Simpson Lumber Company locomotive North Bend seen here on its way to the log dump on Coos River, circa 1900.
Coos Historical and Maritime Museum, Jack Slattery Collection 992-8-0499

on Daniels Creek was established at the site of the Karl Clinkinbeard home. It had a cookhouse, a commissary, and a bunkhouse.

In 1907, Louis Simpson turned over the Daniels Creek railroad and logging operation to a partnership between Bill Vaughn and Jack McDonald. As noted earlier, these two men formed the Coos Bay Logging Company—not to be confused with the original Coos Bay Logging Company formed by Hiram King, Charles Bradbury, and Harry C. Noble in December 1899!

According to Coos County Commissioner Gordon Ross, in 1912 McDonald and Vaughn were logging timber for Simpson in an area cruised by Dennis McCarthy. In the cruise notes, McCarthy indicated that once the timber was removed, the land would be good for agriculture. Since Louis Simpson probably had little interest in livestock, he did not continue the payments for property taxes once the timber was removed. Contrary to the cruiser's comments, no one wanted to buy stump land. Defaulting on the payment of property taxes was a common practice at the turn of the century, and many thousands of acres of cut-over timberland were repossessed by Coos County.

In 1941, Coos County Judge Ervin Peterson, with the help of Coos County District Attorney Ben Flaxel and county budget committee member Everett Messerle, persuaded Senator William Walsh from Marshfield to introduce a bill in the state legislature in Salem, Oregon, that would allow counties to put tax-foreclosed forest lands into a county forest for perpetual harvest, the income from which would help alleviate the tax burden on other properties within the county. Once acted into law, this legislation created the Daniels Creek and the Beaver Hill county forests.

Simpson did not limit his activity to the Daniels Creek region. Around 1908-9 Henry Hoeck purchased the Coos Bay Lumber and Coal Company for the Simpsons and renamed it the Larson Lumber Company. This business arm of the Simpson business,

Simpson logging camp on Daniels Creek. Coos Historical and Maritime Museum, Box 35 000 -D 8 .44

Simpson Lumber Company operation at Tar Heel. Coos Historical and Maritime Museum, Jack Slattery Collection 992-8-0524

which also operated the Beaver Hill Timber Company, built three miles of railroad track to access Simpson timber in the Beaver Hill area. The rail spur was shared with the Smith-Powers Logging Company railroad, which also owned timber in the region. Eventually the Simpson operation at Beaver Hill was sold back to the Henry Hoeck Lumber Company in 1910.

Around the same time, Bill Vaughn extended the Simpson operations to Seelander Creek in the Sumner area. The operation laid about five miles of track, which was used to haul logs until 1935 under Simpson-Vaughn joint ownership.

Louis Simpson also had a logging operation Tar Heel, between the towns of Empire City and Charleston. The rail line used in this area extended quite a distance out into Coos Bay on wooden piling. The main reason for building the trestle out into the bay was likely due to the need to allow tug access to the log rafts without causing damage to the hull. This section of the bay has a fairly wide mudflat before the river channel is reached. As the tide would not cover the area with sufficiently deep water, the log dump built out nearer the channel.

As the need grew for more logs to operate the mill, Simpson also built a railroad into hills at the head of Davis Slough. McDonald and Vaughn again did the logging at this camp. The logs came from property adjacent to the Boutin Tract (later to become the Beaver Hill County Forest). They were transported on the rail line and dumped into Davis Slough for the fourteen-mile tow to Simpson's mill at North Bend.

The Simpsons formed many separate companies as their timber empire expanded. In 1900, Asa Simpson started the North Bend Mill and Lumber Company, and by 1902 had acquired the Coos Bay Logging Company interests and formed the Blue Ridge Railroad and Navigation Company. Simpson also purchased the California Lumber Company mill and locomotive and track. In 1910, the Blue Ridge Railroad and Navigation Company dissolved into the Simpson Lumber Company.

By 1916, most of Simpson's timber on Blue Ridge had been logged. With the passing of Asa Simpson, the line was sold (along with the mill at North Bend and some 25,000 acres) to the Buehner Lumber Company; in 1923

Building the trestle at Davis Slough, circa 1913, for North Bend Mill Company (the old Simpson mill at North Bend owned by Louis Simpson et al). Coos Historical and Maritime Museum, Jack Slattery Collection 992-8-0454

Buehner sold the entire operation to Stout Lumber Company which in turn sold it back to Louis Simpson and Vaughn in 1926. Not quite finished with the timber business, the younger Simpson and Vaughn formed the Bay Park Lumber Company in 1916 and began sawing lumber at the old Porter Mill site in North

Bend. Seven years later, in 1923, Frank Stout took over both the Bay Park Lumber Company and the Buehner Lumber Company operations on the bay.

STOUT LUMBER COMPANY

In the 1850s, the Knapp-Stout Lumber Company was organized in Menominee, Wisconsin. The company's primary business was running a sawmill in the area. James Huff Stout may best be known for founding the University of Wisconsin-Stout, but his fortune was created through harvesting and milling white pine

Sturtevant and Crane Logging at Lampa Creek, circa 1900. Left to right: James Harvey Whitsett, Stewart Whitsett, Lucy Smith, Bonnie Smith, Sarah Smith, and unidentified man.
Bandon Historical Museum, Bates Collection

The Southern Oregon Operation at Sumner, Oregon, circa 1890s. Coos Historical and Maritime Museum, Jack Slattery Collection 992 -8 -0398

forests in the region. As Midwest forests became depleted, Stout moved his sawmilling business to the southern part of the US, where the company stayed for twenty-five years and developed a very successful operation—further adding to Stout's already sizable wealth.

In February 1923, the Stout Lumber Company purchased the interests of the Buehner Lumber Company and moved operations out West. Local papers indicated that Stout would take over Buehner's operations in Coos County in March of that year. It took quite a financial package to acquire the Buehner businesses. Some of the owners of the new Stout Lumber Company were A. L. Payne and Fred Dean of the National Lumber and Manufacturing company in Hoquiam, Washington; W. T. Culver of Luddington, Michigan; and George T. Mickle of Chicago. W. C. Ribenack was the president of the board of directors as well as head of the California and Oregon Lumber Company in Brookings, Oregon. For the most part, the company continued to operate all of Buehner's existing logging camps, railroads, and mill (Mill A) in North Bend, along with another sawmill they purchased directly from Simpson (Mill B). They also used two company steartlers, the Martha Buehner and Frank D. Stout, to carry lumber from Coos Bay to San Francisco.

By the summer of 1923, the company was operating three logging camps at Eel Lake, three at Allegany, and two near Clear Lake. By the end of the year, they were operating both Mill A and Mill B and cutting 500,000 board feet per day. Mill A burned in February 1926. At this time, the company had more than a thousand employees and sufficient timber to keep both mills running for ten years, including extensive timber holdings at the head of South Slough. In 1925 the company built three miles of track to the summit of the ridge, then about seven miles farther south on the route now followed by the Seven Devils Road.

A spur was built off of this rail line that went towards Sacchi's Beach. This rail system accessed about 100 million board feet of fine-grained Port Orford Cedar and Sitka Spruce, as well as another 100 million board feet owned by others tributary to the line.

In late 1928 W. T. Culver bought a controlling interest in Stout Lumber and in 1929 the name was changed to the W. T. Culver Lumber Company. Culver Lumber went into receivership in March 1932.

STURTEVANT AND CRANE

Very little information could be found on this company. In the May 1906 edition of *Timberman* magazine a reference is made to the company moving their railroad to a new location.

SOUTHERN OREGON COMPANY

The story of the Southern Oregon Company starts in 1883 with a trip by Captain William Besse, who entered Coos Bay after sailing around Cape Horn from Massachusetts. After learning of the enormous timber opportunities in area, he returned to New Bedford, Massachusetts, and convinced several investors to purchase sizable timber holdings in the county.

They formed the Oregon Southern Improvement Company, which purchased the Luse sawmill at Empire as well as timberland and farming property. They also purchased 100,000 acres of land owned by the Coos Bay Military Wagon Road Company of San Francisco. By 1887, the company had completed the construction of a big new mill in Empire City, but fell upon difficult financial times. Creditors repossessed the assets. Interestingly, many of the same owners of the Oregon Southern Improvement Company surfaced in the form of the Southern Oregon Company to purchase the properties at a sheriffs auction on the steps of the Coos County Courthouse. The company had a railroad logging operation in the Sumner area; logs were railed to the log dump on Catching Slough, then towed to the mill at Empire.

WESTERN WHITE CEDAR COMPANY

The Western White Cedar Company was organized by A. E. Adelsperger, W. J. Conrad, J. P. Goss, W. L. Forsythe, and R. K Booth. In the summer of 1923, the company built three miles of logging railroad in the Bennett Creek area as well as a rail line up Dement Creek. They used the Coos Bay Lumber Company lines to bring the logs to their mill at Millington, Oregon. Later that year, they sold their logging operation, railroad and timber to the Coos Bay Lumber Company. They were probably one of the largest producers of Port Orford Cedar lumber at the time

Once a large spruce log was opened by wedges on the end of the log, a mechanical jack—called a Griffith jack—was inserted into the crack and the pieces were pried apart, circa 1918. University of Oregon Special Collections and University Archives, Brice P. Disque photographs PH 159 2 -95

chapter four

OTHER PLAYERS

In addition to the individual logging companies profiled on the preceding pages, two additional efforts played important roles in the region's railroad history. The first, the Southern Pacific Railroad, linked the rail lines around Coos Bay to the rest of America. The second, the US Army's Spruce Production Division, constitutes a fascinating episode in the history of logging in the area during World War I.

SOUTHERN PACIFIC RAILROAD

As noted in Chapter 1, the development of Coos Bay as a major industrial center was dependent on the area's abundant natural resources and the transportation of those resources to national and world markets by ocean freight and rail. However, nearly seventy-five years would pass between the establishment of the first coal mines and commercial sawmills around Coos Bay and their connection to the rest of the nation by rail.

Railroad companies of varying sizes desired to reach Coos Bay as it was the only deep-water outlet between San Francisco and Seattle. With its vast natural resources, Coos Bay was a plum waiting to be picked. By 1872 a rail line from Portland had already reached Roseburg at the southern end of the Willamette Valley. Local visionaries—some legitimate, some not—pictured what seemed to be a logical next step: a rail line from Roseburg across the Coast Range to the growing towns of Empire City, Marshfield, and Yarrow on Coos Bay. This would give the local mills and mines on the coast direct rail access to the rest of the nation. Several schemes to forge the link were put forth, but always the physical barriers posed by the rugged coastal mountains and the cost of pushing through a rail line seemed to thwart the plans of even the best financed entrepreneurs of the day. Eventually two big railroad companies were drawn to the opportunity.

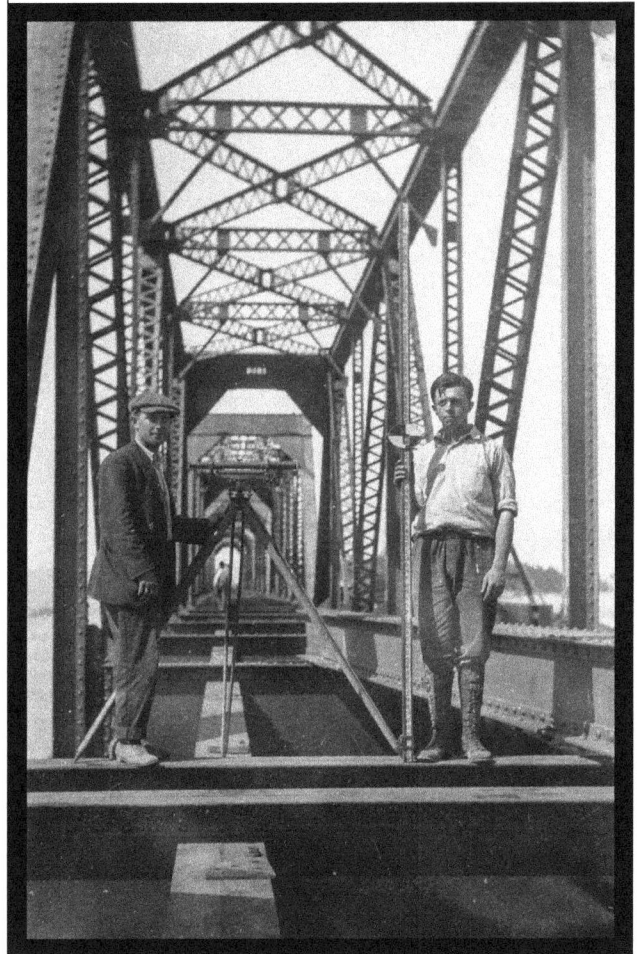

Engineers working on the Southern Pacific bridge crossing Coos Bay, circa 1913. Coos Historical and Maritime Museum PC Box 4 996-36.20

Building the No. 7 tunnel on the SP's Eugene to Coos Bay line.
Coos Historical and Maritime Museum PC Box 4 996-D8

Navigation railroad (CBR&ERR&N) which ran from the bay to the logging centers at Myrtle Point and Powers.

Once the word was out that the Southern Pacific was serious about reaching Coos Bay with a new line, another "real" competitor surfaced. The Oregon Electric Company began surveying a different route—this one from the Willamette Valley town of Eugene, Oregon, to the coastal community of Florence, then down the coastline through Reedsort, and on to Coos Bay. When the SP heard about the plan, it created a new business arm, the Willamette Pacific Railroad Company, and began a furious race to become the first railroad to the coast. In 1906, the SP began constructing its line from Drain, quickly spending $1.5 million on the initial grade and acquiring rights-of-way across private homesteads. In anticipation of winning, it acquired the CBR&ERR&N rail line from Marshfield to Myrtle Point in that same year.

Rumors at the time had it that the Oregon Electric Company was supposedly backed by Great Northern Railroad magnate James Hill along with additional backing from the Northern Pacific Railroad. Both companies were strong competitors of Southern Pacific and both were very well financed. Since there was really no room for two rail companies in Coos Bay, negotiations were undertaken to trade "rail line opportunities" between the two competitors. Reading between the lines, this authors wonders if some, of these negotiations bordered on anti-trust discussions that are illegal in today's business environment. It was finally agreed that the SP's Willamette Pacific Railroad would proceed to survey and construct the rail line to the coast—without competition. As a result, plans for a railroad down the Umpqua River were abandoned despite the SP's sizable investment in that effort, and the railroad was instead built using the Oregon Electric Company's Eugene-Florence-Marshfield route.

It was not until the late 1890s that the Southern Pacific began to survey a rail line into Coos Bay. The company's plan did not follow any of the original routes proposed by early speculators—which tended to focus on a route from Roseburg through the mountains following the middle fork of the Coquille River into Myrtle Point. Instead, the SP developed a route starting at Drain, Oregon, proceeding west across the Coast Range, then dropping down and paralleling the Umpqua River to the town of Reedsport on the Pacific, before turning south to Marshfield and tying into the Coos Bay, Roseburg and Eastern Rail Road and

The team constructing the line over the mountains and down the Siuslaw River faced significant challenges. The surveyors encountered difficult terrain where the only feasible alternative was to bore tunnels through the mountainside. In fact, the rail line from Eugene to Coos Bay passes through nine separate tunnels (the longest 4,183 feet in length). Mastering the rugged topography of the Coast Range also required building many bridges and trestles to cross small streams and major waterways. East of Swisshome, Oregon, for instance, the railroad bridges the Siuslaw River six times; another bridge spans the Siuslaw just west of Cushman.

The challenges did not stop when the railroad reached the coast. Since the goal was Marshfield, the SP had to build a section along the shore of Coos Bay, including a long bridge spanning the bay itself. Here the company hit another problem. Several of the good people of Marshfield and North Bend sent a petition to the US Secretary of War objecting that the proposed bridge across a major shipping channel would interfere with navigation and commerce in the upper portion of the bay. While the complaint was being studied, the SP made an alternative plan to build the line around the east side of the bay, connecting with the CBR&ERR&N line near C. A. Smith's mill at Bunker

The scene pictured above occurred on May 24, 1912, less than one hour after the city council of North Bend ratified the decision to allow the Southern Pacific to build a line across their town heading south along the shoreline to Marshfield in order to connect with the old CBR&ERR&N line to Coquille and Myrtle Point. Shown driving the first spike of the new railway is North Bend mayor Louis J. Simpson, while C. J. Millis, a representative of the Southern Pacific, dashes a bottle of Coos Bay cream on the rails. Also pictured are Captain McGenn of the *Breakwater*. Peter Loggie, C. S. Winsor, J. G. Mullen, A. H. Derbyshire, L. F. Falkenstein, Dr. Bartle, J. G. Horn, George D. Mandigo, H. G. Kern, J. F. Grubbs and other prominent men of North Bend. The track laying was followed by a band concert and general celebration. Coos Historical and Maritime Museum, Jack Slattery Collection 992-8-0904

Arrival of the first train from North Bend Depot, 1916. Coos Historical and Maritime Museum H31 S2-963-83G

While construction of the Southern Pacific bridge across Coos Bay created a direct link with the Willamette Valley, many marine accidents happened as steamers and barges navigated the narrow opening in the bridge. The *Martha Brehner* is shown after it hit the SP bridge at Coos Bay, March 8, 1924. Coos Historical and Maritime Museum, PC Box 4 996-36.26

Hill. Eventually, however, the Secretary of War denied the complaint and the SP proceeded with the construction of a bridge spanning Coos Bay.

There are three draw/swing bridges on the SP route from Eugene to Marshfield: one crossing the Umpqua River at Reedsport, one at Coos Bay, and a small one at Coalbank Slough at the south end of Marshfield near Bunker Hill. The swing bridge crossing Coos Bay is reported to be the longest swing-span in North America. Its construction in 1913 was considered quite a feat.

The first train from Eugene to Coos Bay arrived in August 1916. A railroad "Jubilee" was held to celebrate the event August 24, 25, and 26 in North Bend. Coos Bay now had its long-sought direct link to the rest of America after forty-five years of having only "local" rail service in and around the Coquille Valley and the bay.

Billions of board feet of lumber and other wood products were hauled over the SP line between 1916 and 1985, when the Southern Pacific received permission to abandon all track past the old Georgia Pacific plywood plant in Coquille. By 1989, the last of the tracks and trestles were removed and the grade became a bike/walking path for recreationists. However the line from Coquille, Oregon, to Eugene remains open to this day—primarily to serve the Roseburg Lumber Company plywood plant in Coquille.

Southern Pacific Railroad construction on the Eugene-Marshfield line crossing Tenmile Creek located some ten miles north of Coos Bay. Coos Historical and Maritime Museum PC Box 4 996-D72

Building the approach and railroad bridge for the Southern Pacific crossing
at Coos Bay, circa 1913. Coos Historical and Maritime Museum PC Box 4 996-36014

Building the turnstile swing bridge for the Southern Pacific Railroad crossing of Coos Bay, circa 1913.
Coos Historical and Maritime Museum PC Box 996-36.16

Spans 2 through 7 of the Southern Pacific bridge crossing Coos Bay, circa 1913
Coos Historical and Maritime Museum PC Box 4 996-36.5

A large spruce log being split or "rived" at the Spruce Production Division operations in Raymond, Washington, circa 1918. University of Oregon Special Collections and University Archives, Brice P. Disque photographs, PH159 2-93.

THE SPRUCE PRODUCTION DIVISION OF THE US ARMY, 1917—1918

On April 6, 1917, the United States became involved in the "War to end all Wars"—World War I. This was a new kind of conflict, fought with new types of weapons, including tanks, submarines machine guns, poison gas, and—most important for the history of timber in the Northwest—airplanes. These early planes were flimsy affairs, made mostly of wood, wire, and canvas. Wing spars and fuselage frames were wood. Laminated wood was used for the propellers. Sitka spruce was the species of choice for airplanes of the day because of its strength, low specific gravity (it is a relatively light weight wood), and long, tough fibers that resist splintering and provide maximum stability.

Lumber was desperately needed for the Allies' fast-growing air fleets, and a good deal of it would come from Oregon's forests. In 1916, the Pacific Northwest was already the primary supplier of aircraft quality wood to Britain, France, and Italy. Local mill operators of Coos County were no strangers to supplying the armed forces. But as the War went on, it became apparent that Pacific Northwest private mill operators and loggers could not meet the burgeoning demand. In 1917, demand from the Allies had rocketed to 10 million board feet per month, and production of spruce that summer totaled less than one-third of the demand from the Army Air Corps. The country was in a real pinch. As a result, the US Army decided to help in a very direct way, forming a Spruce Production Division within the Signal Corps to increase the supply quality spruce and Douglas-fir wood for the Allies.

Part of the reason for the local mill's inability to produce the requisite lumber was a general labor strike in the woods led by the Industrial Workers of the World (IWW), commonly known as the "Wobblies." The IWW was joined in the strike by the American Federation of Labor (AFL). In May 1917, Generals "Blackjack" Pershing and James G. Harbord convinced a talented retired officer, Brice Disque (he had retired from the army, but when war was declared, planned to "re-up" and take his place in defense of Europe), to delay his re-enlistment and instead work undercover to assess the labor problem out West and determine ways to increase lumber production in the Pacific Northwest.

Brigadier General Brice P. Disque. On November 6, 1917, then-Colonel Disque was installed as commander of the Spruce Production Division. Disque died in 1960. University of Oregon Special Collections and University Archives, Brice P. Disque photographs

The Army used five-ton trucks to haul the rived spruce from the forest. Here the truck navigates a wooden road in Raymond, Washington University of Oregon Special Collections and University Archives, Brice P. Disque photographs PH 159 2 -80

Pershing knew that the army did not need a uniformed officer to investigate the labor issues in Oregon and Washington. Disque reluctantly undertook this not-so-glamorous assignment and within a few months reported that the labor/management impasse was stalled. He also suggested a solution: Make soldiers into loggers. He proposed establishing a new operation within the US Army Signal Corps for the sole purpose of providing the Army with Sitka spruce and Douglas fir from the coastal forests of the Pacific Northwest—the spruce for airplane production, the Douglas fir for ship construction. The new unit's general assignment would be to build short-line railroads into the forests in Oregon and Washington, fell the giant spruce and fir trees, and bring them out to the local mills for cutting into the required lumber dimensions. As it turned out, Disque's vision was almost complete, except for the necessity of the federal government to build or retool several local sawmills.

On September 29, 1917, Disque was reinstated into the Army as a Lt. Colonel. His first assignment was to meet with the major players in the labor disputes in the Pacific Northwest woods. While the start-up of this military cause seemed noble and important, the local union factions saw the soldier/loggers as tantamount to strikebreakers. Over a period of a couple of months and with the application of national loyalty to the war effort, Disque was able to quiet the strikers and allow the army to go to work getting the logs out of the woods.

On November 6, 1917, Colonel Disque was given command of the new military unit he had proposed. It was called the Spruce Production Division, and was headquartered in the Yeon Building in Portland, Oregon. Army logging camps soon began to spring up in the coastal forests from Washington's Olympic Peninsula to Coos Bay, Oregon. These early camps were, for the most part, large tent camps. Once lumber began to flow, more permanent barracks and wooden structures were constructed.

As Disque had predicted, recruiting experienced woodsmen posed something of a problem: Recruits generally signed up to fight the "Huns" in Europe, not

Only the largest, straightest, defect-free spruce trees were harvested to fabricate airplane parts. University of Oregon Special Collections and University Archives, Brice P. Disque photographs PHI59 2-56

Airplane spruce being sawn at the Monarch Mill in north Portland, circa 1918. University of Oregon Special Collections and University Archives, Brice P. Disque photographs PHI59 4-41

swing an axe in Oregon! Regardless, Disque made his request for experienced woodsmen to the Army commanders, and recruits with logging experience or who had worked in the Forest Service began to flow into his unit. By May 1918, the Spruce Production Division had 10,317 soldiers, including both commissioned and noncommissioned officers.

Since the spruce logs sought for airplane parts had to be free of knots and other structural defects, only the largest and oldest trees were harvested. At the outset, the Spruce Division engineers believed that a combination of short-haul truck roads and a short-line rail system would provide the best transportation network to get these large logs to the local mills. The original rail plans were extensive, including thirteen railroads throughout the coastal forest of Oregon and Washington covering 173 miles of main line and 181 miles of spurs. But there was a problem to be solved on the truck side—the trucks were not large enough

to haul the giant logs. The logs had to be split or "rived" in order to be hauled from the woods. The quality of the spruce logs that were used during WW I would make the sawmill owners of today green with envy.

The first logging camp and rail line built by the Army was on the Olympic Peninsula in Clallam County, Washington. The vast forests of the region seemed perfect for the operation. Unfortunately, no spruce would be forthcoming from the project. With some thirty-six miles of main line track completed, seventy miles of logging railroad grade leveled, the Port Angeles mill 70 percent complete, machinery en route to the Lake Pleasant mill site, and 150 million board feet of logs in various stages of harvest, all activity was abruptly halted on November 11, 1918, when the Armistice was signed between Germany and the Allies. Of particular interest was a subsequent

Congressional investigation of the $4 million spent on the Clallam operation as extravagant and wasteful. After months of hearings, the committee released Disque from any charge of wasteful wrongdoing.

Nonetheless, during its fifteen months of existence

the Spruce Production Division's accomplishments were considerable. As reported in the publication the History of the Spruce Production Division, spruce production jumped from 2.9 million board feet per month to 22.1 million board feet during its operation. Another important part of the story about logging railroads in Coos County is the fact that the Coos Bay District of the Spruce Production Division was the last logging camp and rail line built by the Army before the Armistice.

As detailed in the newspaper article that follows, considerable time, effort and money were also poured into developing the spruce forests at Beaver Hill in Coos County. On September 11, 1918, two months before the War's end, the Coos Bay Times reported:

130 SOLDIERS HERE TO OPEN RAILROAD WILL BE 500 BY NEXT MONTH IN BOUTIN SPRUCE TRACT
G.B. Herington is in Charge of Work Which Will Open Timber for Half Thousand Loggers

Arrival last night by special train of 130 soldiers, an advance contingent of about 400 more to come during the next 30 days for the construction and repair of the railroad which is to tap the Boutin spruce tract by Beaver Hill spur, brought to Coos Bay the realization that it is rapidly becoming an encampment of soldiers at work in boosting spruce production for airplane building.

These 500 railroad builders are only the advance workers for approximately 500 other men, it is stated authoritatively, who will work in the spruce camps which are to be opened at the conclusion of railroad construction work, which is hoped for by the end of October and perhaps earlier.

TO LIVE IN TENTS

Early this morning the detachment breakfasted behind the old Southern Pacific Depot in Marshfield, cooking and eating in the open air, and proceeded via a special train, composed of three sleepers, 2 baggage cars, one flat car with a truck and automobile, a caboose and car of construction timbers to Beaver Hill where the striking of tents will take place today. G. B. Herington, a former Southern Pacific official now in government service, but still a civilian, is

district supervisor of lathes work and arrived with the train to take charge of the work.

Lt. Paul Morgan is in charge of the 130 men who comprise the 142nd spruce squadron ju s t made up at Vancouver, Washington. Other officers are Lt. Hunter, Lt Jones, Lt S. B. Degnan, medical officer and Lt. C. A. DeCamp. The latter engineering officer was one of the men who in 1912 worked with the party locating the Coos Bay line. He was somewhat surprised at the growth which the city has shown since he was here six years ago.

A.L. Downs, Southern Pacific trainmaster and A.D. Wick, traveling passenger agent, arrived last night with the party to see that all arrangements were made.

The train crew and the train which took out the cars to Beaver Hill will be held therefor the present till suitable quarters and other equipment and supplies arrive.

LEASE LENEVE LINE

Lease on the railroad logging line of the Moore Mill and Lumber Company which reaches from Leneve on the Coquille River several miles into the woods, will be made as the result of negotiations now in progress it is said. This will be connected up with the Beaver Hill spur extending now several miles from the main line to Beaver Hill.

DOLLAR A YEAR MAN HERE

Major G. E. Breece, also of the spruce division, arrived on the Bay last night with C. H. Edwards and was today inspecting the mills with Lt John F. McGovern, who is in charge of spruce inspection in this district. Major Breece is one of the dollar a year men working for the government.

It was reported earlier by the newspaper that the Spruce Division wanted to buy the Boutin timber outright, but Frank Boutin had set his price too high. As the story goes, Boutin owned one-third of the timber, but he represented the interests of the other two investors. After some haggling, they finally settled on a stumpage rate contract, but still far apart in value—Boutin wanting $7 per

Coos County Spruce. Coos Historical and Maritime Museum, Jack Slattery Collection 992-8-0164

thousand board feet, the government offering $5. Being a time of war, there was no real argument as the government would simply commandeer the timber, so the deal was sealed without much negotiation.

The first order of business for the local Division was to get a railroad into the Beaver Hill area. This required construction or reconstruction of the old CBR&ERR&N Beaver Hill Branch line's extensive system of low trestles across the bottom lands. Once the rail lines were built, the Army's locomotives were brought on site, and the government began ordering large quantities of lumber with which to build barracks, mess halls, and other support buildings. In addition, orders were placed for food and housing supplies to support the troops at Beaver Hill. An order for 1.5 million board feet of lumber went out to the local mills (the bill, according to a local newspaper, was upwards of $40,000).

As it had done in other locations, the Army undertook to re-tool one of the local mills to cut lumber specifically for its needs. It took over the operations at the Coquille Lumber Company in Coquille, Oregon, where the Division built a two-story barracks to house 52 soldiers and two officers assigned to running the mill. On the lower floor were shower baths, toilets and laundry tubs. The main lounging room faced the Coquille River and contained a pool table, piano, and athletic equipment. The building was heated with hot water. A mess hall just outside the mill served as a restaurant for the civilian employees as well the recruits.

Since the Smith-Powers Logging operation in the Powers area had access to high quality spruce timber, the Army dedicated some of its recruits to working alongside the company's private loggers. They were also involved in the construction of the rail lines to access the company's timber. The same was true for the Buehner Lumber Company operations at Eel Lake. On September 24, 1918, the *Coos Bay Times* reported:

> The old Klondike coal mine near Beaver Hill has been opened by the government to supply fuel for the eight Shay engines which will be used by the government

A typical tent camp of the Spruce Production Division of the US Army Signal Corps, circa 1917. University of Oregon Special Collections and University Archives, Brice P. Disque photographs

Army recruits falling a large Sitka spruce on the southern Oregon coast. These fine-grained old growth spruce trees were perfectly suited for the airplane industry of the day, 1918 University of Oregon Special Collections and University Archives, Brice P. Disque photographs

Spruce Production Division Locomotive No. 13. Coos Historical and Maritme Museum, Jack Slattery Collection 992-8-297

Large Sitka spruce logs being hauled to a local mill from the Beaver Hill operation, 1918. University of Oregon Stadden Collection 23-ST25

Constructing the low trestle across the lowland conecting the Southern Pacific line with the Beaver Hill Camp, October, 1918. University of Oregon Special Collections and University Archives, Brice P. Disque photographs

The barracks for the men at the Beaver Hill Camp were the typical tent-roof structures with wooden floors and sides, 1918. University of Oregon Special Collections and University Archives, Brice P. Disque photographs

Constructing the mess hall at Camp Warnick at Beaver Hill, October, 1918. University of Oregon Special Collections and University Archives, Brice P. Disque photographs

Riving Port Orford cedar, Coos County, circa 1917. University of Oregon Special Collections and University Archives, Brice P. Disque photographs PH159 5-50

*in logging the Boutin timber. John Swanson has
been appointed to take charge of the construction
end of the mine and Hugh McLain (who originally
opened the Klondike mine 20 years earlier) and J. H.
Flanagan will have charge of the coal business end.
Civilian labor will be used in the mine and offers of
$5.20 per day have gone out to the community.*

The Armistice had a big impact on the Beaver Hill
operation also. As reported by the Coquille Herald on
November 15, 1918:

*The spruce project started by the Portland Lumber
Company on government contract at Beaver Hill
has been ordered stopped. Withdrawal of the troops
will begin at once. There has been expended a
vast amount of money on the greatest project even
contemplated for the Coos Bay District. Most
of the railroad had been completed, four of the sidings
were in, 20 donkey engines and 10 pile drivers are on
the ground, with a great amount of other machinery
and logging equipment. Much of the building work
has been started, a mess hall with seating capacity
for 600 men was just completed, the first meal to be
served in it was breakfast Monday morning (next
week). Bunk houses and other cantonment buildings
were in process of building many near completion.
Several bridges had been built. It is estimated that the
money spent on the project runs into the hundreds of
thousands [of dollars].*

The production hopes of the Beaver Hill/Coos Bay
Division did not come to pass. The War was over within
two months of starting the operation. However, the
Division had built 1.5 miles of railroad and prepared
another 2.6 miles of grade. The timber on the Boutin tract,
however was hardly touched. After the Armistice, the rail
line was sold to the Conlogue and McKenna operation,
but demand for spruce had obviously plummeted. The
government stores and supplies inventoried at the Beaver
Hill operation were sold to local merchants.

Spruce timber on the Boutin Tract at Beaver Hill, 1918.
University of Oregon Special Collections and University
Archives, Brice P. Dique photographs PH159 5-58

Steam engine with logs. Smith-Powers Logging Company Locomotive No. 1 Coos Historical and Maritime Museum, Jack Slattery Collection 999-10.37A

Appendix

THE LOCOMOTIVES OF COOS COUNTY

Prior to the Civil War, America's logging operations were concentrated in the Great Lakes region of the Midwest. Due to the nature of the soils and climate of that area, logging was generally done in the winter months when the ground was frozen and ice-covered rivers provided for excellent skidding by horse teams. An open winter—one that was warmer than normal or where the freeze was light—could be a disaster for local loggers and their customers, the sawmills.

The first logging locomotive, the story goes, was devised around the mid-1860s by two men named Wright and Pier, loggers along the Clarion River north of Brooksville, Pennsylvania. The Civil War was in full swing and demand for lumber from the Union forces was high. Wright procured a small boiler from a nearby town and a local blacksmith outfitted a small rail-car with the engine. The first American logging locomotive was born. They called it Little Wonder. Power was delivered to the drive wheels by means of an eight-inch belt running from a pulley on the engine shaft to a pulley on one of the drive axles; the two axles were connected by cranks and side rods.

The advantages of railroad logging quickly became apparent throughout the industry. With appropriate ballast in the roadbed and the use of piling to cross swampy areas, the logger's season could be greatly expanded.

Two basic types of locomotives played major roles in the woods:

ROD LOCOMOTIVES

The conventional "rod" locomotive gets its name from the side "rod" or metal bar that connects all of the drivers (driving wheels) to the steam cylinder. In order to keep in alignment with the rod, the drivers had to be fixed straight in place, one in front of the other, and were unable to turn like the drivers on geared locomotives. This limited the degree of curves that rod locomotives could safely navigate. The more drivers a rod locomotive had, the less it could tolerate the sharper curves. The rod kept the drivers on one side moving in unison. In general the drivers on the rod locomotives were larger than that of the geared type which gave the rod more speed on the straight tracks, but they struggled on any grade over 2 percent. Rod locomotives had other drawbacks, too: Not only could they not handle the sharp turns and steep climbs that typified logging railroads in the mountainous terrain out West, but they also proved quite hard on tracks and were a bit unstable on the cheaply laid tracks that were often used in loggers' railroads.

The Baldwin Locomotive Works of Philadelphia, Pennsylvania, is most notable for its production of thousands of rod locomotives. The company only constructed five geared locomotives from 1913-1915. It is not known why their geared endeavors were so brief and presumably unsuccessful. Little is known about these locomotives. None of them came to Coos County, Oregon.

A number of rod locomotives built by the Baldwin company found their way into the hands of railroad loggers in Coos County, including Cody Lumber Company engine No. 4 (shop #32288), Port Orford Cedar Company engine No. 120 (shop #43213), and a number of Smith-Powers Logging Company locomotives: No. 7 (shop #57013), No. 101 (shop #38271), No. 102 (shop #38965), No. 193 (shop #38968), No. 104 (shop #55911), No. 120 (shop #43213), and the oldest Baldwin in the fleet No. 5 (shop #9150) manufactured in 1887. The Coos Bay, Roseburg and Eastern Rail Road and Navigation Company ordered the first Baldwin to find its way to Coos County in 1887 (shop #4054).

GEARED LOCOMOTIVES

Ephraim Shay, who engaged in logging operations in Haring, Michigan, during mid-1870s, is credited with inventing a new steam locomotive design that

The Locomotives

Smith-Powers Logging Company Locomotive No. 1 SN489.
Coos Historical and Maritime Museum H8-989-D37A

Smith-Powers Logging Company Locomotive No. 2 SN1827.
Coos Historical and Maritime Museum 992-8-0294

Coos Bay Lumber Company Locomotive No. 7 SN1841.
Coos Historical and Maritime Museum Box 1977-101-39

THE SHAY B
Built: 1887
Manufacturer: Shay 2, Lima
Shop Number: 169
Weight: 28 tons
Track Gauge: Standard
Fuel Type: Coal

Ownership History
Stimson Mill, Marysville, WA
Winchester Bay Lumber, Reedsport OR
Smith-Powers Logging #3, Powers, OR
Schroeder and Aasen, Norway, OR, leased
Coos Bay Lumber #3, Powers, OR
Marion Bennett Powers, OR
Henry Sorensen, McKinleyville, CA
Scott Wickett, Centrailia, WA for restoration

SMITH-POWERS #1
Built: 1895
Manufacturer: Shay 2, Lima
Shop Number: 489
Weight: 36 tons
Track Gauge: Standard
Fuel Type: Coal

Ownership History
Henry Hoecke, Marshfield, OR
Larson Timber of Simpson
Salt Lake and Mercury #2, Fairfield, UT
M.T. O'Connell Lumber, Winlock, WA
Smith-Powers Logging #4
Coos Bay Lumber #4

BUEHNER #1
Built: 1903
Manufacturer: Shay 2, Lima
Shop Number: 765
Weight: 37 tons
Track Gauge: Standard
Fuel Type: Wood

Ownership History
North Bend Mills #1, North Bend, OR
Stimson Lumber #1, Empire, OR
Buehner Lumber, Allegany, OR
Zimmerman, Wells & Brown, Portland, OR
Forcia & Larson #1, Noti, OR
Snellstrom Brothers Lumber #1, Vaughn, OR
Globe Lumber, Globe, OR boiler only
Scrapped

SMITH-POWERS #2
Built: 1903
Manufacturer: Shay 2, Lima
Shop Number: 765
Weight: 37 tons
Track Gauge: Standard
Fuel Type: Wood

Ownership History
Coos Bay Lumber and Coal #2
C.A. Smith Lumber and Manufacturing #2
Smith-Powers Logging #2, Powers, OR
Zimmerman, Wells & Brown, Portland, OR
Columbia Contract, St. Helens, OR
Scrapped

COOS BAY LUMBER #7
Built: 1895
Manufacturer: Shay 2, Lima
Shop Number: 1841
Weight: 36 tons
Track Gauge: Standard
Fuel Type: Coal

Ownership History
Gardiner Mill #1, Gardiner, OR
C.C. Carter Lumber, Myrtle Point, OR
England and Cyphers Lumber #1, Gaylord, OR
Coos Bay Lumber #7, Powers, OR
Lawson Cypress Lumber, Byerle, OR
Scrapped

revolutionized logging railroads throughout the nation. As Shay himself told the story in a letter written on November 11, 1912:

> In 1873, I owned and operated a saw mill in Haring, Michigan, getting out bridge and building timber. Business was dull and prices barely paid expenses. I was compelled to reduce costs or quit. Logging costs $3.50 per thousand from stump to mill, using horses and logging wheels, the best known plan at that time. I built a tramway using maple for rails, procured a double-truck car, and tried the plan out; Resulting in reducing costs of logging to $1.25 per thousand, but the cars would catch the horses on the downgrade and sometimes killing them. Brakes were impractical. Logs ran from 12 feet to 75 feet in the same load, and trucks had to be separated to suit the load. We usually let the cars run down alone.
>
> I finally concluded to try a light locomotive and with the help of a local repair shop, did so. It worked, but destroyed my track, while the cars weighing twice as much did not injure it. I could see that if I could convey the power to the trucks, instead of the customary drives, the track would stand up. I could not use the engine on wet rails while snow was falling so during the winter, so I rebuilt it, conveying the power as best I could to trucks. It worked better, and for six more winters I did the same rebuilding each time, as experience seemed to require, until the cylinders only were left of the original engine. All of this work was done by me and my blacksmith, and was crude to the extreme, but it drew my logs from anywhere and all places, saving much labor and was extremely profitable. Of course, castings and most machine work I had to go to shops for, although I had a lathe, drill and some machine tools
>
> My friends remonstrated with me for spending so much time and money on such a crazy idea and, in fact, they really thought I was a little cracked and did not hesitate to say so. Actually, I was tired of it myself and would have been pleased to give it up, but the constant ridicule to which I was subjected angered me and I was obliged to continue in self-defense to make it a success.
>
> One consoling feature was that I was all the time making more money from its use, and I could get more for my timber than my neighbors. My customers knew rain, bad roads, etc., it did not deter me from logging and their lumber would be out on time.

Geared locomotives, as the name implies, use gears to connect the steam cylinders to the wheels, producing more constant pulling power than "rod" type locomotives. The most common geared locomotives were the Shay, Climax, and Heisler engines. Each was made by a different company with different means of implementing geared power to their drivers.

Geared locomotives were the "4-wheel drive" versions of the rod locomotives. Lighter and smaller than their rod cousins, they could climb steeper grades (in excess of 10 percent) and operate on lighter, smaller rails, even those that were crooked and poorly maintained. Gear locomotives were perfect for loggers out West.

The lifespan of a section of track into a timber stand lasted no longer than the time it took to remove the timber. Once the logs were taken to the mill, the rails were pulled up, moved to a new area, and relaid for the purpose of removing the next stand of timber. The constant handling of the rails often required straightening before they were placed back into service—they were never returned to their original condition, but good enough for the logger. The idea was to "get in and get out" as quickly and as cheaply as possible. Unlike the passengers transported on mainline railroads, the logs and rocks carried on logging railroads didn't care how bumpy or uncomfortable the ride was.

SHAY LOCOMOTIVE

The Shay consisted of two or three vertical steam cylinders positioned on the right side of the engine just forward of the crew cab. The piston rods were attached to a crankshaft similar to that used in today's automobile engines. Attached to either end of the crankshaft were drive shafts that extended

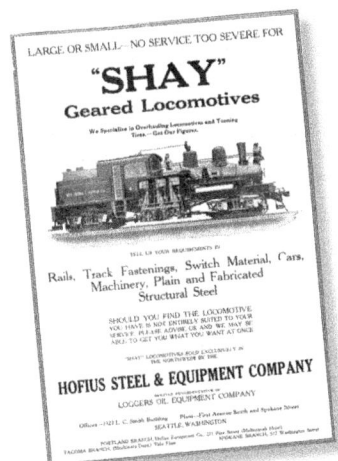

Shay locomotive advertisement from a 1919 issue of The *Timberman* magazine. Oregon Historical Society 35172

George Chaney operation at Glen Aiken Creek, circa 1927
SN1944 Coos Historical and Maritime Museum 992 -8 -0197

Buehner Lumber Company Locomotive No. 2 SN2302
Allegany, Oregon. Oregon Historical Society 35078

Coos Bay Lumber Company Locomotive No. 6 SN2542.
Coos Historical and Maritime Museum 992-8-0198

CODY #2
Built: 1907
Manufacturer: Shay 2, Lima
Shop Number: 1999
Weight: 36 tons
Track Gauge: Standard
Fuel Type: Wood/Coal

Ownership History
Cody Lumber Company #2
Moore Mill and Lumber Company #2,
   Leneve, OR
Conlogue Brothers #2, Charleston, OR
McKenna Lumber Company, Charleston,
   OR
Baldridge Lumber Company, Winchester
   Bay, OR Scrapped

NO. 1944
Built: 1907
Manufacturer: Shay 2, Lima
Shop Number: 1944
Weight: 28 tons
Track Gauge: Standard
Fuel Type: Wood/Coal

Ownership History
Smith-Powers Logging Company #1,
   Powers, OR
Coos Bay Lumber Company #4
E. Hall Chaney #1 Coquille, OR
George H. Chaney Logging Company,
   Coquille, OR

BUEHNER #2
Built: 1910
Manufacturer: Shay 2, Lima
Shop number: 2302
Weights: 37 tons
Track Gauge: Standard
Fuel Type: Wood

Ownership History
Simpson Lumber Co. #2 (1st), Empire, OR
   circa 1913 McDonald & Vaughan Co. #2,
   Marshfield, OR
North Bend Mill & Lumber Co. #2, North
   Bend, OR (1916) Buehner Lumber Co.
   #2, North Bend, OR
(4-1-1924) Stout Lumber Co. #2, North
   Bend, OR Scrapped

SIMPSON #3
Built: 1910
Manufacturer: Shay 2,
Lima Shop Number: 2303
Weight: 18 tons
Track Gauge: Standard
Fuel Type: Wood

Ownership History
Simpson Lumber Co. #3 (1st), Empire, OR
North Bend Mill & Lumber Co. #3, North
   Bend, OR
(1916) Buehner Lumber Co. #3, North
   Bend, OR
(circa 1924) Stout Lumber Co. #3, North
   Bend, OR Scrapped

RANDOLPH #1
Built: 1912
Manufacturer: Shay 2,
Lima Shop Number: 2518
Weight: 36 tons
Track Gauge: Standard
Fuel Type: Coal

Ownership History
Randolph Lumber Company #1
(Seeley and Anderson #1) Bandon, OR
   Robert Dollar Lumber Company Bandon,
   OR
North Bend Mill and Lumber Co. #4, North
   Bend, OR Stout Lumber Company #4,
   North Bend, OR. Scrapped

COOS BAY
LUMBER #6
Built: 1912
Manufacturer: Shay 2, Lima
Shop Number: 2542
Weight: 42 tons
Track Gauge: Standard
Fuel Type: Wood/Coal

Ownership History
Smith-Powers Logging Company
Coos Bay Lumber Company Scrapped

to a gear box on the outside of each wheel. The left side had no gearing or cylinders. The boiler was located to the left of center of the entire frame. This was necessary for the location of the cylinders and made the machine look "lop-sided."

CLIMAX LOCOMOTIVE

A second major maker of geared engines, the Climax locomotive, consisted of two steam cylinders from which piston rods extended and attached to a transmission located under the center part of the engine frame.

Connected to the front and rear of the transmission were drive shafts that ran along the center line of the engine below the boiler, cab, and fuel bunker. The drive shafts were connected to gear boxes in each truck.

A Climax locomotive advertisement from a 1902 issue of The Timberman magazine. It was manufactured by the Climax Manufacturing Company of Correy, Pennsylvania. Oregon Historical Society 35176

HEISLER LOCOMOTIVE

The Heisler consisted of two steam cylinders positioned in a "V" under the boiler. The piston rods came out of the cylinders and attached to a crankshaft located under the center of the boiler. Attached to either end of the crankshaft below the center line of the engine were drive shafts. On two truck models, the drive shaft attached to a gear box that was located on each truck's wheel set located furthest from the center of the engine frame. Power was then supplied to the other wheel set on the truck with an out-board tie rod connecting two wheel sets together.

SCHENECTADY LOCOMOTIVE
ALCO (AFTER MERGER IN 1901)

CUYAHOGA LOCOMOTIVE

A Heisler advertisement from a 1910 issue of The Timberman magazine. Oregon Historical Society 35174

Coos Bay, Roseburg and Eastern Rail Road and Navigation Company Locomotive No. 2, an example of an engine built at the Cuyahoga Locomotive Works 1878, SN unknown. The engine was brought to Coos County in 1893. Coos Historical and Maritime Museum, Jack Slattery Collection 992-8-0280

WHYTE'S SYSTEM OF LOCOMOTIVE CLASSIFICATION
circa 1900

Class	Front Idlers	Drivers	Rear Idlers	Name
0-4-0	0	4	0	Four-wheel switcher
0-6-0	0	6	0	Six-wheel switcher
0-8-0	0	8	0	Eight-wheel switcher
2-6-0	2	6	0	Mogul
2-6-2	2	6	2	Prairie
2-8-0	2	8	2	Consolidation
2-8-2	2	8	2	Mikado
2-8-4	2	8	4	Berkshire
2-10-0	2	10	0	Decapod
2-10-2	2	10	2	Santa Fe
2-10-4	2	10	4	Texas
4-4-0	4	4	0	American
4-4-2	4	4	2	Atlantic
4-6-0	4	6	0	Ten Wheeler
4-6-2	4	6	2	Pacific
4-6-4	4	6	4	Hudson
4-8-2	4	8	2	Mountain
4-8-4	4	8	4	Niagara
4-8-8-4	4	16	4	Union Pacific "Big Boy"

2603

Built: 1912
Manufacturer: Shay 2, Lima
Shop Number: 2603
Weight: 42 tons
Track Gauge: Standard
Fuel Type: Coal

Ownership History
Randolph Lumber Company #1, Bandon, OR
Puget Sound Sawmills and Shingle Company #1, Concrete, WA
W. H. Peters Logging Company #1, Ethel, WA
Malone Creek Logging Company #1, Roseburg, WA Scrapped

COOS BAY LUMBER #7

Built: 1913
Manufacturer: Shay 2, Lima
Shop number: 2650
Weights: 42 tons
Track Gauge: Standard
Fuel Type: Coal

Ownership History
Sugar Pine Lumber Company
Smith-Powers Logging Company
Coos Bay Lumber Company
Scrapped

HUDSON #1

Built: 1918
Manufacturer: Shay 2, Lima
Shop Number: 29663
Weight: 60 tons
Track Gauge: Standard
Fuel Type: Soft Coal

Ownership History
Hudson Motor Car Company #1, Detroit, MI
LaDee Logging Company #1, Estacada, OR
C. M. Christenson Logging Company #1, Kerry, OR
K. P. Timber Company, Kerry, OR leases
George H. Chaney Logging Company, Coquille, OR

NORTH BEND MILL AND LUMBER #1

Built: 1918
Manufacturer: Shay 2, Lima
Shop Number: 297
Weight: 50 tons
Track Gauge: Standard
Fuel Type: Wood

Ownership History
North Bend Mill & Lumber Co. #2978 later #2, North Bend, OR
(1-12-1924) Stout Lumber Co. #2978, North Bend, OR (10-7-1925) Converted to oil burner
McKenna Lumber Co. #2978, North Bend, OR
Conlogue & McKenna Lumber Co. #2978, North Bend, OR
(12-6-1928) Oregon White Cedar Co. #2978, Charleston, OR
Ingham Lumber Co. #2978, Glendale, OR
(4-20-1946) Robert Dollar Lumber Co. #2978, Glendale, OR
(4-1961) San Francisco Maritime Museum Association, Oakland, CA; (stored)
(4-1985) Leased to Bay Area Electric Railroad Association, Rio Vista, CA
Western Railway Museum, Rio Vista, CA
(4-9-2005) Roots of Motive Power, Willits CA

Coos Bay Lumber Company Locomotive No. 9 SN2998.
Coos Historical and Maritime Museum Box H1 977-101-40

COOS BAY LUMBER #9

Built: 1918
Manufacturer: Shay 2, Lima Shop number: 2998
Weights: 42 tons
Track Guage: Standard
Fuel Type: Oil

Ownership History
Warren Spruce Company Spruce Production Division
Spruce Production Division #9
Smith-Powers Logging Company #9
Coos Bay Lumber Company #9
McKenna Lumber Company #9

NO. 3179
Built: 1922
Manufacturer: Shay 2,
Lima Shop Number: 1944
Weight: 42 tons
Track Gauge: Standard
Fuel Type: Oil

Ownership History
Hudson Motor Car Company #1 Detroit, MI
LaDee Logging Company #1 Estacada, OR
C. M. Christenson Logging Company #1
    Kerry, OR
K. P. Timber Company Kerry, OR leases
George H. Chaney Logging Company,
Coquille, OR

NO. 321
Built: 1923
Manufacturer: Shay 2,
Lima   Scrapped
Shop Number: 3211
Weight: 36 tons
Track Gauge: Standard
Fuel Type: Coal

Ownership History
Moore Mill and Lumber Company

Moore Mill and Lumber Company Locomotive SN3211, at Leneve, Oregon, circa 1926. Coos Historical and Maritime Museum, Jack Slattery Collection 0176

NO. 3223
Built: 1923
Manufacturer: Shay 2, Lima
Shop number: 3223
Weights: 36 tons
Track Gauge: Standard
Fuel Type: Coal

Ownership History
Coos Cedar Company # 201
Scrapped at Powers 1954

NO. 708
Built: 1906
Manufacturer: Shay 2, Lima
Shop Number: 708
Weight: 20 tons
Track Gauge: Standard

Ownership History
England and Cyphers Gaylord, OR
Lawson & Cyphers Lumber Company,
    Gaylord, OR
Pacific Steel Company, Irondale, WA
Seattle Car and Foundry, Renton, WA
    Mineral Creek Lumber Company, WA

Climax engine SN708, from the Pacific White Cedar Company, a firm associated with Lawson and Cyphers Lumber Company. Coos Art Museum CC2734B

NO. 1108
Built: 1907
Manufacturer: Heisler 2
Shop Number: 1108
Weight: 37 tons

Ownership History
Defiance Lumber Company, Buckley, WA
James M Neely Lumber Company, Buckley,
    WA
Lawson & Cyphers Lumber Company,
    Gaylord, OR

SMITH-POWERS #5
Built: 1903
Manufacturer: Climax 2
Shop Number: 445
Weight: 35 tons
Track Gauge: Standard

Ownership History
Mann and Montgomery #1, Clifton, OR
Smith-Powers Logging Company #5
Coos Bay Lumber Company #5
John Aasen circa 1925

Smith-Powers Logging Company Locomotive No. 5 SN445 at the McCormac log dump on Isthmus Slough. Coos Historical and Maritime Museum, Jack Slattery Collection 992-8-0190

NO. 1019
Built: 1898
Manufacturer: Heisler 2
Shop Number: 1019
Weight: 14 tons

Ownership History
Gardiner Mill Company Reedsport, OR
Aasen Bros. Norway, OR
John Aasen Norway, OR
Schroeder and Aasen Coquille, OR

A Heisler 2 locomotive of the Smith-Powers Logging Company in 1916. SN1349. Coos Historical and Maritime Museum 992-8-0204

Smith-Powers Locomotive No. 101 SN38271. Coos Historical and Maritime Museum 992-8-0204

Smith-Powers Locomotive No. 103 SN3896. Coos Historical and Maritime Museum, Jack Slattery Collection 0171

Coos Bay Lumber Company Locomotive No. 104 SN55911. Coos Historical and Maritime Museum Box H1 977-10-47

1165
Built: 1909
Manufacturer: Heisler 2
Shop Number: 1165
Weight: 23 tons

Ownership History
Winston-Dear Company, Hibbing, Minnesota Whitney Engineering Co., Tacoma, WA Aasen Brothers, Norway, OR
John Aasen, Norway, OR Schroeder and Aasen, Norway, OR
E. A. Aasen, Reedsport, OR.

1112
Built: 1907
Manufacturer: Heisler 2
Shop Number: 1112
Weight: 37 tons

Ownership History
Lamb Davis Lumber Company, Wenatchee, WA
Wenatchee Valley #101, Wenatchee WA
Great Northern Lumber Company, Wenatchee
Coos Bay Logging used at Greenacres, OR

1124
Built: 1907
Manufacturer: Heisler 2
Shop Number: 1124
Weight: 36 tons

Ownership History
Peninsula Lumber Company, St. Johns
Cowden Lumber Company, Sauk, WA
Coos Bay Logging Company used at Greenacres, OR

SMITH-POWERS # 101
Built: 1912
Manufacturer: Baldwin
Shop Number: 38271
Wheel Alignment: 2-8-2

Ownership History
Smith-Powers Logging Company
Coos Bay Lumber Company #101
Puget Sound and Cascade #101

SMITH-POWERS # 102
Built: 1912
Manufacturer: Baldwin
Shop Number: 38965
Wheel Alignment: 2-8-2

Ownership History
Smith-Powers Logging Company
Coos Bay Lumber Company #101
Clear Lake Lumber Company, Clear Lake, WA

SMITH-POWERS # 103
Built: 1912
Manufacturer: Baldwin
Shop Number: 38968
Wheel Alignment: 2-8-2

Ownership History
Smith-Powers Logging Company
Coos Bay Lumber Company #101
Kern and Kibbe #103
US Army, Pendleton, OR

COOS BAY LUMBER # 104
Built: 1922
Manufacturer: Baldwin
Shop Number: 55911
Wheel Alignment: 2-8-2

Ownership History
Coos Bay Lumber Company
Georgia Pacific #104
Preserved at Coos Bay, OR

COOS BAY LUMBER # 10

Built: 1922
Manufacturer: Willamette
Shop Number: 1
Weight: 70 tons
Fuel Type: Oil

Ownership History
Coos Bay Lumber Company
Cobbs Mitchell Lumber Company #104, Valsetz, OR
Valsetz Lumber Company # 104, Valsetz, OR
Zidell Explorations, Valsetz, OR
Scrapped 1952

Locomotive No. 10 SN68548, an example of a Schenectady locomotive (2-8-2 t), built December 1930 for the Coos Bay Lumber Company. Coos Historical and Maritime Museum Box H1 977-101-46

COOS BAY LUMBER # 11

Built: 1929
Manufacturer: Alco
Shop Number: 68276
Weight: 84 tons
Track Gauge: Standard
Fuel Type: Oil
Wheel Alignment: 2-8-2t

Ownership History
Coos Bay Lumber Company #1

Coos Bay Lumber Company Locomotive No. 11 SN 68276. Coos Historical and Maritime Museum Box H1 977-101-56

According to Lyle McCulloch, Sr., who often operated # 11, this engine hauled sixty-three loaded log cars on a forty-four-mile trek from Powers to the mill at Isthmus Slough. It pulled its last train to Myrtle Point's centennial in July 1962. In 1967, Georgia Pacific donated # 11 to the Pacific Southwest Railway Museum Association. It left Powers on June 17, 1968, on its own wheels, but derailed three days later and was declared "untrackworthy" by the Southern Pacific. It was renovated and renamed for John A. "Nick" Nichols, one of the volunteers. In 1976, # 11 was used in filming Universal Pictures' MacArthur with Gregory Peck. At last report, it was on display at a museum at San Ysidro.

COOS BAY LUMBER # 12

Built: 1930
Manufacturer: Alco
Shop Number: 68487
Weight: 84 tons
Wheel Alignment: 2-8-2t

Ownership History
Coos Bay Lumber Company

Coos Bay Lumber Company Locomotive No. 12 SN 68487. Coos Historical and Maritime Museum Box H1 977-10-50

Simpson logging operation at Daniels Creek, 1910.
Coos Historcal and Maritime Museum 992-8-0457

Epilogue

My goal at the outset of this project was to document the history and location of the railroads of Coos County, a subject about which little if anything has been written to date. My admiration for the early pioneers grew as I realized how truly daunting the isolation of the region was. These men and women faced enormous challenges transporting and utilizing the bountiful timber and coal resources they discovered; they accomplished incredible feats without the advantages of modern technology and equipment. Determination and foresight were their tools and the forest and mining resources of Coos County were their target.

The coming of the railroad to Coos County was a key step in the growth of this section of the Oregon coast. The region was separated from the rest of the nation by the steep topography of Oregon's Coast Range. Access to the region from the ocean was also difficult due to the necessity of crossing the dangerous river bars under sail. Once the area's resources became known, sawmills and coal mines began popping up around Coos Bay and the mouth of the Coquille River at Bandon. The forests and mines close to these water courses were quickly exploited by the early entrepreneurs, and it soon became clear that unless a new method was found to reach further inland, growth in the area would stall. Railroads satisfied the transportation needs of both coal miners and loggers and Coos County continued to flourish.

Even today, locals complain about the isolation of Coos County and the difficulty and expense of getting local resources to market. Little does the current population know of the trials that the early pioneers faced in bridging the real isolation of the County! The railroads and the investment in the Coos Bay Military Wagon Road were the major factors opening the "backcountry" of Coos County and allowing the population to develop in small communities such as Dora, Fairview, Powers, Norway, and Lakeside, as well as larger towns like Coquille, Bandon, and Myrtle Point.

In 1916, the Southern Pacific arrived in Coos Bay and forever changed the shape of the industries of the region. Now local products from the area could reach the ever-growing interior markets of the nation. The new rail line could also bring new items to the expanding population of the county. In addition, people living in the towns alongside the rail line could now travel to Portland and points east more quickly and reliably. Without the railroads, the growth of Coos County would have been curtailed for decades.

As with any enterprise, it is difficult to single out any one person as the sole reason behind an area's success, but the communities of Coos County owe a debt of gratitude to those intrepid early settlers who came here, brought their capital and their families, and built railroads into the vast timber stands and coal fields throughout the region.

Since little physical evidence remains today to remind us of the existence of the early railroads, an unexpected surprise occurred when I drove the old railroad grades atop Blue Ridge. I was searching for evidence of the logging operation of the old McDonald and Vaughn Logging Company, which operated on the Ridge in the early 1900s. Today the Bureau of Land Management owns much of that land, and I discovered that as the BLM began developing the area the modern engineers simply followed the old railroad grades established by the logging company 100 years before. As I traveled the many miles of road grade atop the Ridge, sweeping curves bordered by tall 80-year-old Douglas-fir trees, my imagination quickly gave rise to an image of a steam locomotive coming around the gentle turn pulling a load of logs headed for the ride down the long incline to the valley below.

I could almost "hear the whistle blowin'."

Two railroad carts or "trucks" were used by early loggers in Coo's County. Each truck had four wheels held together either by the logs chained to each other or by a small log pole that swiveled as the carts made turns. Coos Historical and Maritime Museum 989-P 137

Bibliography

SOURCE MATERIALS

BOOKS AND ARTICLES

Abdill, George B. *This Was Railroading*. Seattle: Superior Publishing Company, 1958.

Abdill, George B. *Pacific Slope Railroads—from 1854 to 1900*. Seattle: Superior Publishing Company, 1959.

Abdill, George B. *A Locomotive Engineer's Album—the Saga of Steam Engines in America*. Seattle: Superior Publishing Company, 1965.

Adams, Kramer. *Logging Railroads of the West*. Seattle: Superior Publishing Company, 1961.

Alexander, E. P. *Iron Horses: American Locomotives 1829-1900*. New York: Bonanza Books, 1941.

Anonymous. *Glancing Back*, vol. 1 p. 206. Coos Bay: Coos-Curry Pioneer and Historical Association, 1971.

Anonymous. *The Heisler Locomotive 1891-1941*. Benjamin F. G. Kline, Jr., 1982.

Austin, Ed, and Tom Dill. *The Southern Pacific in Oregon*. Edmonds, WA: Pacific Fast Mail, 1987.

Beckham, Curt. *Tall Timber Tales*. Myrtle Point, Oregon: Myrtle Point Printing, 1989.

Beckham, Curt. "Early Coos County Loggers," *The Sentinel* (newspaper), July 13,1988.

Beckham, Dow. *Stars In The Dark: Coal Mines of Southwestern Oregon*. Coos Bay: Arago Books, 1995.

Beckham, Stephen Dow. *Coos Bay—The Pioneer Period 1851-1890*. Coos Bay: Arago Books, 1973.

Beckham, Stephen Dow. *The Land of the Umpqua: A History of Douglas County, Oregon*. Roseburg, OR: Douglas County Commissioners, 1986.

Case, George Baxter. T*he History of the Port of Coos Bay 1852-1952*.

Edinburg, TX: A thesis presented to the graduate school of the Pan American University (Master of Arts), 1983.

Cook, Richard J. *Superpower Steam Locomotives*. San Marino, CA: Golden West Books, 1966.

Culp, Edwin D. *Stations West: The Story of the Oregon Railways*. Caldwell, ID: The Caxton Printers Ltd., 1972.

Diller, J. S. *Mineral Resources of Southwestern Oregon*. Washington D.C.: United States Geological Survey, 1914.

Dodge, Orvil, *Pioneer History of Coos and Curry Counties*. Salem, OR: Capital Printing Co., 1898.

Douthit, Nathan. *The Coos Bay Region 1890-1944: Life on a Coastal Frontier*. Coos Bay: River West Books, 1981.

Douthit, Nathan. *A Guide to Oregon South Coast History: Including an Account of the Jedediah Smith Exploring Expedition of 1828 and its Relations with the Indians*. Coos Bay: River West Books, 1986.

Douthit, Nathan. *The Coos Bay Region 1890-1944*. Coos Bay: Coos County Historical Society, 2005.

Gibbons, William H. "Logging in the Douglas-fir Region," United States Department of Agriculture Bulletin No. 711 (1918).

Goodyear, W. A. *Coal Mines of the West Coast, 1877*.

Greif, Steve. *A Century of Coos County Railroads*. Unpublished Manuscript, June 1974.

Hauff, Steve, and Jim Gertz. *The Willamette Locomotive*. Portland, OR: Oso Publishing, 1977.

Koch, Michael. *The Shay Locomotive: Titan of the Timber*. Denver: World Press, Inc., 1971.

Labbe, John T., and Vernon Goe. *Railroads in the Woods*. Berkeley: Howell-North, 1961.

Mahaffy, Charlotte L. *Coos River Echoes*, Portland: Interstate Press, 1965.

Nevin, Hattie. *Reflections of a Logging Camp Cook*. North Bend, OR: Wegferd, circa 1980.

Peterson, Emil R., and Alfred Powers. *A Century of Coos and Curry: History of Southwest Oregon*, Coquille, OR: Coos-Curry Pioneer and Historical Association, 1952.

Phillips, Jerry. *Caulked Boots and Cheese Sandwiches: A Forester's History of Oregon's First State Forest*. Coos Bay: Butler's Pronto Print, 1996.

Puter, Stephen Douglas. *Looters of the Public Domain*. Portland: Portland Printing House, 1908.

Ranger, Dan, Jr. *Pacific Coast Shay: Strong Man of the Woods*. San Marino, CA: Golden West Books, 1964.

Robbins, William G. *Hard Times in Paradise Coos Bay, Oregon, 1850-1986*. Seattle: University of Washington Press, 1988.

Ross, Gordon. *Gordie: The Life and Times of George Ross, Jr. 1905-1995*. Coquille, OR: self published, 2000.

Stone, Boyd. *The Way it Really Was in Coos and Curry Counties*. Coquille, OR: The Coquille Valley Sentinel, 1993.

Taber, Thomas T. III, and Walter Casler. *Climax-An Unusual Steam Locomotive*. Morriston, NJ: Railroadians of America, 1960.

United States Army. *History of the Spruce Production Division*. Portland: Kigham Stationary and Printing Company, 1920.

United States Geologic Survey. *Nineteenth Annual Report, Part III Economic Geology*. Washington, DC: Government Printing Office, 1899.

United States *Geologic Survey. Twenty-Second Annual Report, Part III: Economic Geology*. Washington, DC: Government Printing Office, 1902.

Wagner, Judith, and Dick Wagner. *L J: the Uncommon Life of Louis Jerome Simpson*. North Bend, OR: Bygones, 2003.

Webber, Bert, and Margie Webber. *Railroading in Southern Oregon and the Founding of Medford*. Fairfield, WA: Yegalleon Press,1985.

Weitzman, David. *The Brown Paper School Presents My Backyard History Book*. Boston: Little, Brown,1975.

West, Victor. "Logging Locomotive No. 104," Unpublished Manuscript in Historical Series No. 2, Coos Curry Museum, 1980.

Williams, Richard L. *The Loggers*. New York: Time Life Books, 1976.

Willingham, William F. *Army Engineers and the Development of Oregon: A History of the Portland District, U.S. Army Corps of Engineers.* Portland: The District, 1983.

NEWSPAPERS AND MAGAZINES

Significant research for this book was done by combing through periodicals of the day. Newspapers that yielded many nuggets included early issues of Coos Bay's newspapers, the *Harbor, News, World,* and *Times,* as well as the Coquille *City Herald* and Bandon *Western World.* Magazines and journals included many old issues of The *Timberman,* as well as *The American Lumberman, Pacific Pride, Pacific News, Forestry History,* and the *Oregon Historical Quarterly.* Readers who want to know more about this time, this industry, and this place are encouraged to spend time thumbing through these invaluable, often fascinating publications.

COMPANY PUBLICATIONS

Evans Products brochure.
Baldwin Midland Champion brochure.
Port Orford Cedar Products company brochure, 1929.

WEBSITES

http://www.apawood.org/plywoodpioneers/pdfs/PPA_17.pdf
http://www.Climaxlocomotives.com/history/index.php
http://www.udayton.edu/~hume/Steam/steam.htm
http://www.shaylocomotives.com/data/lima

PERSONAL INTERVIEWS AND CORRESPONDENCE

Richard Hansen, private correspondence.
Interview with Nellie Palmer, Myrtle Point, Oregon, 2006.
Interview with Steven Pappajohn, President, Methane Energy, Coquille, Oregon, 2006.

Two railroad carts or "trucks" were used by early loggers in Coo's County. Each truck had four wheels held together either by the logs chained to each other or by a small log pole that swiveled as the carts made turns. Coos Historical and Maritime Museum 989-P 137

Smith-Powers logging at South Slough. Coos Historical and Maritime Museum 992-8-0174

Index

About the Author

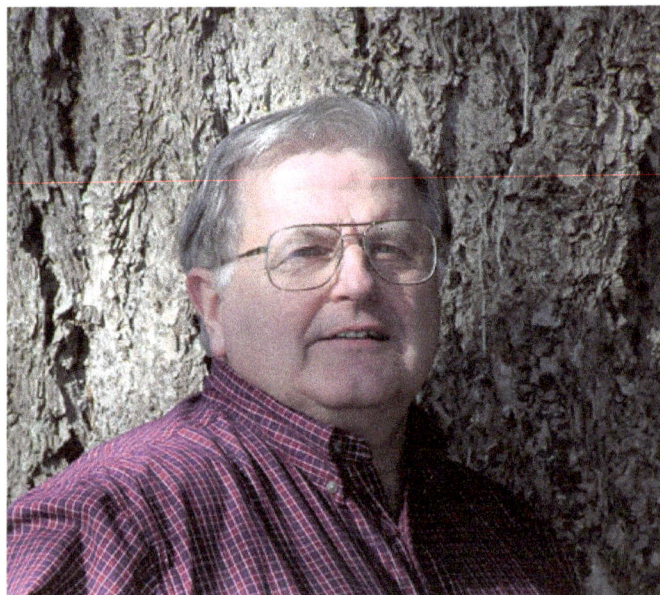

William A. "Bill" Lansing is the former President and CEO of Menasha Forest Products Corporation headquartered in North Bend, Oregon. He and his wife Ann have made their home in North Bend since 1969, raising two sons in the area. Bill grew up in the country near the small town of Colfax, California. He graduated from Sierra College in Rocklin, California, majoring in mathematics and forestry, and worked summers as a firefighter for the California Division of Forestry—an experience that lead him toward a career in forestry.

Following graduation from Sierra, he attended Humboldt State College in Arcata, California, receiving a Bachelor of Science degree in Forest Engineering in 1967. Bill then went on to the Yale Graduate School of Forestry in New Haven, Connecticut. Upon graduation from Yale in 1969 Bill went to work for Menasha in North Bend—first as an intern, then as a Research Forester. The Menasha position was intended to last only until, in his words: "until something better came along"... but Menasha was a good "fit" and nothing did!

After thirty-seven years at Menasha, in what he thought would only be a transition job, Bill retired in April 2006. In anticipation of making the transition into retirement. Bill decided he would commit more of his time to documenting some of the local history of Coos County, Oregon. *Can't You Hear the Whistle Blowin'* is his second book about the area; his first *Seeing the Forest for the Trees: Menasha Corporation and Its 100-Year History in Coos Bay, Oregon*, was published in 2005.